The Executive Parent

by
S. P. Hersh, M.D.

SOVEREIGN BOOKS • NEW YORK

Published by Sovereign Books
A Simon & Schuster Division of
Gulf & Western Corporation
Simon & Schuster Building
1230 Avenue of the Americas
New York, New York 10020

Designed by Irving Perkins

Manufactured in the United States of America
10 9 8 7 6 5 4 3 2 1

Library of Congress Cataloging in Publication Data

Hersh, Stephen P
  The executive parent.

  Includes bibliographical references and index.
  1. Parenting—United States.   2. Executives—United
States.   I. Title.
HQ755.8.H47   301.42′7   79-16164

ISBN: 0-671-18428-8

To J. L. H. and our dynamic trio

Acknowledgments

The old saying is true! But this time *three* women must be recognized.

First, I wish to thank Madelyn Larsen, Senior Editor at Sovereign Books, for it was she who discovered me. From a series of quotations in *Business Week*, Ms. Larsen tracked me down and challenged me to write this book. Without her actions and persuasiveness, given my other responsibilities, I would never have undertaken this project. Second, she introduced me to Moira Duggan, who worked patiently and helpfully reviewing manuscript as my first audience and editor. Ms. Duggan's suggestions greatly facilitated the timely completion of the project.

The third woman I warmly acknowledge is my wife, Jean Lehrke Hersh. I now understand the many acknowledgments by male authors to their wives. Without her support I could not have written this book while continuing my other professional activities. That support meant her first encouraging me to respond to Madelyn Larsen's challenge and then volunteering to assume the major, ongoing responsibilities for children and home while I engaged in the necessary activities that are involved in writing a book. One needs space and time; the processes of synthesis and creating do not fit into scheduled mini-time segments. As an artist she understood this better than I did before we launched into this project. There is more to thank her for. She listened to my struggles and my ideas, gave freely of her own ideas, was consultant on all parts of the book, and was a reader of even rough, first-draft material.

Many other persons contributed to this book. Some provided inspiration by sharing their experiences, particularly Robert Stubblefield, M.D., director of the Silver Hill Foundation in New Canaan, Connecticut, and president-elect of the American Academy of Child Psychiatry. Others, such as T. Berry Brazelton, M.D., served as role models for me, teaching the importance of making time in our schedules to convey professional knowledge and "secrets" to the public as an important effort of advocacy on behalf of children and their families.

Contents

Foreword

The Executive Parent is designed to enhance the quality of life for executives as they endeavor to fulfill two demanding roles—nurturing parent and successful professional. By underlining each role with insight, Stephen Hersh has given the executive the opportunity to feel more fulfilled. This is a worthy and timely book.

The women's movement has led the way. It has voiced the hunger in half our society for a better opportunity to participate equally and rewardingly with the other half in their professions. As women have exposed the conscious and unconscious putdowns which sap them of strength and rewards in their professional lives, they have also brought to light the need for a parallel understanding of the rewards in family life and parenting.

Not only do we need such an understanding for professional women, but also for executive men who have long since tended to abdicate many of their opportunities for nurturing and being nurtured within the family. This book will serve toward such a purpose. Dr. Hersh is a talented and inspired executive as well as a highly respected psychiatrist. The professional demands on him are double those of most people. As a result, he has worked against and thought a lot about the demands on his emotional energy which might interfere with his family life. Married to a gifted and dedicated artist, they both have shared the work and excitement of raising their three children. When Steve comes home at night, all his family rushes to greet him at the door—not out of a sense of duty or from any sense of deprivation, but with the expectation that he is there *for them*. They surround him with accounts of their day—and, to my surprise, ask him to tell them about his. This impressed me, and saddened me. I realized that I'd missed out with my own children in this way. As I listened to his "dressed up" accounts of what could have been a pretty routine professional day, I realized that he was sharing with them a window into the excitement of being a physician who deals with each patient individually and of being in a position to plan for some important programs for people all over the country. As "their" visitor, they politely asked me what I had done all day. I tried to explain it to them in a way they could understand. (I'd been in fairly dull meetings all day.) As I endeavored to keep their interest, I found that I, too, began to dress up my day. All of a sudden, my day began to seem more worthwhile. This style of communication had managed to make me turn stress into excitement. Steve's insights are just such an attempt—to urge executives, male and female, to treasure this union of the excitement in their professions with the rewards of sharing that excitement with a family.

But this isn't an easy job, and it does demand the work of self-examination from most high-powered people. I have practiced pediatrics in Cambridge, Massachusetts, in the midst of talented and successful professionals at Harvard and the Massachusetts Institute of Technology. I have learned a lot from them. But they drive themselves and their families hard. Their children are under internal and external pressures. The internal pressures seem to come from a combination of the genetic endowment for success and the expectation of success that goes with it. The internal pressures are more subtle. They are all around us in Cambridge. The atmosphere crackles. Positive reinforcement for success surrounds every child. But with it also goes the fear of failure, the costly expectation of perfectionism, and the realization that maybe you aren't always perfect. Some children, by the ages of five and six, are dogged by poor self-image. For such children, the mild learning disabilities which normally show up in the first and second grades are no longer mild nor are the children easily reachable.

This culture is not unique to Cambridge. Wherever I go, I am impressed with this same ambience—with its emphasis on achievement and relative inattention to the cost. Most executives, male and female, have probably paid some of this cost along the way in their own development. With the increasing awareness of the rewards of family life which we seem to have been ignoring in the past, parents who read this book will be looking for better solutions for themselves and their families. They will come to this book aware of their internal drives and ready to protect their children from the expense of parental ambition.

Children need to share and participate in the excitement of an intense, driving parent—not to be denied the rewarding side of his or her drive. There is no way to really protect them from this side of our personalities, except by the worse deprivation of a relationship with us. They need to be aware of the cost of such a personality structure because they themselves are likely to be in the same mold. In order to pass on such an understanding, we need to understand ourselves—how and why we function the way we do. This excellent volume is a step toward that goal.

T. Berry Brazelton, M.D.
Children's Hospital Medical Center
Harvard Medical School

Preface

Since 1960, at least a hundred books have been published in the United States on the subject of parenting. Is another one really necessary? Shouldn't caring for the child be as natural a process as "making a child"?

It's true that both processes are in a sense "natural," but this does not equate with simple or uncomplicated or even unchallenging. The role of being a parent is more complex than ever before in history. There are new problems and new dimensions to age-old problems. Both parents and children are looking for guidance. In adding to the literature I hope to offer guidance of a very specific sort.

This age of easy communication and rapid travel sees more men and women working as executives. These are the senior administrators, managers, and policymakers in those inward and outward spiraling structures called corporations, foundations, government agencies, and universities. For such individuals, responsible and satisfying parenting is a major challenge.

Without prior conscious planning, I've found myself to be

one of these individuals. My own experiences as parent, psychiatrist, and executive provide the motivation for writing this book. To my knowledge, no other volume about parenting written specifically for the executive person exists. Such a volume is long past due.

Until relatively recently, most adults engaged in parenting by necessity. From the mid–nineteenth century to the present, rapid changes in our technology and economic structures removed much of that necessity. For example, food and goods could be purchased with increasing ease, so that a large family was no longer necessary in the home to grow and manufacture what was needed; systems of income maintenance and support, such as insurance and social security, were developed, obviating the need of adults to rely on their children for material assistance. During the same period of history, various more effective forms of contraception were developed, culminating in the near perfect control provided by the Pill. For the first time in human history, the creation of children became truly an act of choice available to most people through means other than abstaining from intercourse. Together, these developments produced the current social conditions in which the raising of children has become more a matter of choice than it had been at any other time in human history. Simultaneously, in the developed nations such as ours, the reasons for having children have become more abstract, and more subtle.

Family structures and parenting roles have altered with the changing necessity for children. Obvious indicators are the increased number of single parents (once married or never married), of divorced and remarried parents, and of the various forms of foster parenting and adoption. Various social changes are influencing, indeed buffeting, the family structures, roles, and all the individuals involved. These changes include the logarithmically increasing sociocultural developments of the last eighty years, during which rapid technological development has brought us from horse and man power to steam, atomic, and solar energy; from fear of epidemics to concern about the cost of maintaining a person on life-support machines; from low to high population density; and from a reasonable abundance of goods to intense consumerism and waste.

Along with the change in family structure we have experienced dramatic modification in the work roles of parents. More and more parents are entering jobs away from the home. This applies particularly to women: Between 1970 and 1976 the number of working women with children under eighteen years of age increased 10 percent.[1] Many of these jobs, because they are away from the home and the immediate community, are difficult to explain and to involve children in.

Working parents, including those in executive roles, join the ranks of the many adults who feel uncertain about the importance of what they are and what they do. Modern markers of such uncertainty include the dramatic growth of soul spas such as Synanon and regain-control movements such as EST, as well as faddism about nutrition and exercise. Unfortunately for the young, the uncertainty of adults extends to their functioning as parents. About this we should all be concerned.

Change in the current reality is possible. Our species possesses an incredible capacity for coping with all forms of change and stress. I refer to this as *human tensile strength*. The most basic responsibility of educators, healers, and religious leaders is to enhance that human tensile strength. As much as possible, individuals and families should be aware of and develop their own coping capacities. They should refer to psychiatrists and other healers for assistance only when needed. This ability of knowing when to seek help is something that can, beginning in childhood, be taught. Simultaneously, those physicians, educators, and clergy consulted should work as much as possible toward reinforcing the physiological, physical, and emotional integrity and autonomy of the individuals and their families who seek help.

The family, no matter what form it takes, is also critical to attaining the needed movement away from uncertainty. I reject the currently popular interpretation that the increase in divorce, remarriage, co-parenting, and parents going to work all herald the death of families. To quote a forceful statement by Margaret Mead[2]:

> We must act to interrupt the runaway belief that marriages must fail, that parents and children can't help but

be out of communication, that the family as an institution is altogether in disarray. There are still far more marriages that succeed than ones that fail; there are more parents and children who live in trust and learn from one another than ones who are out of touch; there are more people who care about the future than we acknowledge.

This book is deliberately written for those who live with special privileges, expectations, and stresses. In most societies, those with the greatest control over resources significantly determine not only the direction of the society but also the values and mores of its citizens. Today's executives are such individuals. They pay a price, however, for their special privileges through dealing with expectations and stresses whose quality, quantity, or duration is known to few others. I write to them in the hope that my sharing of information, perspectives, and strategies for coping will reinforce their sense of integrity and autonomy and their belief that the existence of the family is necessary to fulfill the demonstrated human needs for community and continuity.

S. P. HERSH, M.D.
Somerset, Maryland

The
Executive
Parent

1
The Rewards of Caring

This may seem a strange way to begin, but I want to tell you about a visit I made recently to a horse-breeding farm. The farm does business in excess of a million dollars yearly selling show-quality saddle horses to buyers throughout the country. It integrates many trades and technologies and produces beautiful, strong, prizewinning animals. The manager of the operation functions as an executive in every sense of the word.

Since the horses, young and old, are seen in terms of their economic value, the farm can certainly be termed a business. However that does not preclude a genuine, deep caring for the animals on the part of the staff. Indeed, that caring—or love, if you will—seems to contribute to the astounding success of this particular farm in comparison to others with equal financial backing and technology.

I was amazed at the manager's description of the breeding

3

farm's operations. The horses, even before conception—from the selection of dam and sire—are given every chance for success. Throughout their uterine life and into their equivalents of infancy, childhood, and adolescence, they receive more comprehensive physical and dental care (with emphasis on prevention) and more individually oriented education than do most children of even our wealthy citizens. Those who care for and parent these animals are in continuous contact with each other, going over technologies and techniques and holding what the manager calls "white coat" sessions where they try to solve any problems they may be having with each other, with the farm management, and with their wards, the horses. "It's all necessary, and mostly common sense," says the manager. The farm, in short, is an example of business methods applied to the production and nurturance of healthy, talented offspring, horses that can be sold at very high prices.

At least since the latter part of the nineteenth century in the United States, advocates of a more self-conscious attention to the health, nutrition, and development of our children have been espousing elements of what that farm manager so comfortably presented as both common sense and the working reality of his breeding operation.[1] At one time these advocates had a more obvious case than they do now: Children had value as economic units, although this point never was articulated in such direct terms. The activities of children in the daily economy and material operation of the family made a positive difference to its functioning. An example is the help farm children gave with the seasonal harvest (the original reason for the summer vacation from school). Today, with the disappearance of clear economic roles for children, that motivation has disappeared. Furthermore, popular writings often express negative economic attitudes toward children, as when they cite figures on the cost of raising children from birth through college—$40,000 to $75,000 per child.[2]

Year after year advocates plead on behalf of children and adolescents, presenting to Congress evidence based on sound scientific research. The results of this chronic advocacy are federal support programs that fall far short of real commitment to solving the problems of the child population—accident prevention, immunization, nutrition, education, and mental health. Peculiar, isn't it? Somehow years of advocacy by selected citizen and professional groups have not been able to do for children what the saddle-horse industry is doing for horses.

As individuals, children certainly are considered important. However, the understanding of their value *as a group* to those beyond the immediate family tends to be limited. A gut-level belief in their importance to the future, as well as to the current social fabric, does not exist throughout our adult population. Such a belief does not fit comfortably with our cultural traditions of individualism, ownership, and family independence.

However, I believe there is reason to hope for a change in this situation. The past decade has seen a new concept established in our national consciousness: the idea of ecological systems, of the interrelatedness of things. If we abandon negative thinking about the cost of children and instead view children positively for their contribution to the ecological health of families and communities, we can arrive at an understanding of their true worth to society as a whole.

I would like to open some fresh perspectives on the business of caring for and about our children. Though these perspectives may well have interest to adults in general, I address myself particularly to executives who also are parents. It is my experience that executives would like to acquit themselves as well at home as they do in the workplace, yet their jobs very often leave them abstracted of mind and too short of time and temper to deal resourcefully with the needs of their children. This conflict is real, but I believe it can be lessened by a better understanding of the real issues and rewards of parenting.

EXECUTIVE AND PARENT

The well-functioning executive is one who consistently succeeds in meeting the demands of the workplace. Such a person has tremendous capacities and strengths, which can and should be mobilized in the parent role. Yet we see that somehow these skills too often are not mobilized by executives within their own families. The results can be a household full of strangers—or worse. There may be such noticeable family dysfunctions as poor school or work performance, vandalism, drug or alcohol abuse, running away, desertion, bewildered disappointment, separation, and divorce. I submit that such outcomes contribute significantly to the mental health problems in this country. I further submit that most of these problems do not have to occur, that indeed they can be completely avoided or their extent and severity significantly reduced.

One author has pointed out that a majority of the executives he studied saw themselves as confident, competent, and open-minded.[3] When you add to such traits the executive's ability to focus attention, to control impulsive behavior, to approach problem situations from an analytic, solution-oriented perspective, to deal with input overload, and to engineer time, only a few things are lacking to complete the description of an ideal parent. Just add a genuine fondness for children and young people, empathy, and a capacity for love, and one has that desired parent.

EVENTS AND THEIR CONSEQUENCES

For humans, the events which unfold from conception through all subsequent developmental stages are major determinants of adult functioning. These stages encompass events which may be described as *physiological* (the internal workings of the body), *physical* (the growth, development, size, and shape of the body), *cognitive* (experiences, conscious reactions to these experiences, and intellect), *psychological* (thoughts, feelings, moods, and patterns of reaction to internal and external events), and *social* (all experiences with others both individually and in groups). Just as the groundwork for future physical health is laid in childhood and adolescence, the groundwork for attitudes and behaviors is formed then, too.

Our attitude toward aging, for example, is one that is formed in childhood and is carried over into the rest of our lives. Experiences children have with truly old people set, when positive, a very different intellectual and emotional tone than those produced by uncomfortable, anxiety-provoking exposure. The explanations children get when they wonder about "very old" people and the reactions children observe in others (particularly in their parents) create in them either positive or negative attitudes toward the aging process. These experiences determine a child's future capacity for working and coexisting with the aged in a positive way and the attitude that the child will have as an adult toward his or her own aging process.

Clearly, early events in all our lives influence our future health and level of functioning. Children who survive childhood become the adults who contribute to, or who drain from, the social and economic system of their society. The following two sketches, derived from real events, illustrate these statements about the relationship of childhood functioning and experiences to later behavior.

Sketch 1: Father and Son

"Jump!" the man said. It was his father. The boy was ten years old, strong, nice-looking, and of average intelligence. He stood in the hayloft door on the barn's second floor.

"Jump! Don't be chicken-shit. I'll catch you!" his father repeated more insistently.

The boy jumped. His father stepped aside, letting the boy crumple on the ground. Silence. The child wasn't dead; the wind was knocked out of him, the dull throb of his badly sprained ankle not completely registering.

His father broke the silence yelling at him: "That'll teach you. And don't you ever forget it, not to trust anyone in your life. No one, do you hear! Never." His father walked off, leaving the boy on the ground.

Angry at being hurt, at this break of trust, and unable to say anything, the boy lay on the ground for a while. He was confused. His anger grew into a feeling of rage as he realized his powerlessness. He should have known better than to trust his father. He had had such experiences before.

Oh how he hated (yet loved) that man. Who could he believe if not him? How should he behave in the future?

As the boy grew, he unfortunately experienced many other episodes which increased his sense of helpless anger. These experiences also taught him that trusting was dangerous. He wasn't sure why he began the behavior that resulted in his being sent away, but setting fires made him feel better. He felt stronger, and the flames (he'd watched them from a distance) seemed to make his anger go away for a little while. He was caught setting these fires; the places they sent him away to were supposedly for treatment but didn't make much difference. At the beginning, in the first few places he was sent to, some people worked hard with him, trying to help. He kept testing their interest in him and whether they could really be trusted. His need to test was much greater than anyone's tolerance for his testing, a testing that involved more fires, stealing, rages, and running away. Eventually they gave up on him and he floated: detention homes, part-time work, jails, drinking, and more jails. The story could end in several ways; his ended in prison with a blow to the skull from a fall down a flight of metal stairs.

Sketch 2: Mother, Son, and Family

"I was a little over a year old when they began to take me to hospitals and clinics. . . . Almost every doctor . . . labeled me a . . . hopeless case. Many told mother I was mentally defective. . . .

"She refused to accept this truth. . . .

"Four years rolled by. . . . I could not speak . . . nor could I sit up without support. . . . I seemed . . . to be convulsed with movement, wild, stiff, snake-like movement that never left me, except in sleep. My fingers twisted and twitched . . . my arms twined backwards and would often shoot out suddenly . . . my head lolled and sagged sideways. I was a queer, crooked little fellow."[4]

This quotation comes from the autobiography of Irish author and painter Christy Brown. Birth injury produced in him the condition known as cerebral palsy. His mother and his family, along with the accidental discovery that he could have fine motor control over his left foot and toes, helped him emerge from the prison of his distorted body and its uncoordinated movements. Years of patient hard work combined with the support and optimism of his family allowed him to take advantage of his few abilities. Eventually, advanced physical therapy and education techniques supplemented the other efforts. He gained enough control to write and speak. He learned to discipline and organize his own thoughts. By the age of twenty-three, he had published his autobiography. A decade later *Down All the Days* was published, a novel hailed as a "literary miracle." The novel is a stormy, irregular, and brilliant book. Christy Brown has followed both books with collections of poems and paintings, and he subsequently moved into his own home. These extraordinary accomplishments highlight how his fate was dramatically altered by the events of childhood. Those events determined the difference between vegetation and death in an institution or the existence (not without pain and storm) he has ended up having, an existence which has contributed to so many.

PRIDE AND PARENTING

For most of us, our existence through our work lives can be compared to a spoon dropped in porridge: An impression is made while the spoon is lying there on the surface, but once it has sunk beneath the surface, to all appearances the spoon no longer exists, it gives no external hint of its continued presence in the substance of the porridge. Be we humble or grand and powerful in our careers, with rare exceptions, we leave little behind after our departure in the way of easily identifiable traces.

We pour so much of our attention and our energies into our work lives, yet we are haunted by the metaphor of the spoon and the porridge. For despite all the rituals, awards, and incentives with which we surround ourselves, rarely will our work have any lasting significance. This factor may partly explain why many of us existing in the modern technocracy have a deeply felt need for some sense of continuity. We need to feel involved with something that frees us from our biological selves and our relative insignificance. Although our strivings may be as important or unimportant as any other events in the universe, without a sense of context and values our efforts become relatively meaningless.

Having points of reference based on the human structures provided by culture, religion, and individual interactions with other people allows us to resonate with the beauty and drama of life experiences. Without such reference points, the challenges of life can quickly produce feelings of anxiety, even panic. The insistent needs that others make known to us serve us well, although we rarely attach much importance to washing dishes or taking someone shopping. For most people, families provide on a daily basis the majority of our human reference points. The family is a vessel that holds safe our values and our personal sense of continuity. It is the depository of oral history, traditions, myths, and knowledge. It provides us with a continuum, binding us into a system that has a past and a future beyond our immediate reach.

That continuum which the family provides has as its essence the process of caring for children—parenting. The effects of parenting are clear and observable throughout our lives. The two sketches just presented serve as real but extreme examples. Most of us, fortunately, do not encounter such challenges. Rather, the happiness or unhappiness, the perceived success or failure of our children, profoundly affect us as parents. They also affect other family members and even the future lives of those not yet born. The effects of parenting reverberate long after our deaths in the personality and behavior of the individuals who survive us, adding to the continuity granted us within the family. Indeed, the extent and quality of parenting goes beyond each family to the community. Cumulatively it serves as a major determinant of the future of our culture.

ON USING AUTHORITY

Parents and executives—do these two roles relate, and if so, how? As parents we have great authority and power. Over infants and toddlers our power is obvious, given their total dependence on us for survival and our comparatively greater physical and intellectual strengths. At a more subtle level, it is not power and authority that we exert but rather influence. Recall your child's use of voice or hand and face gestures; recall your child's sense of humor and mischief, of sadness and beauty. All these behaviors resemble in some form or another the behaviors and reactions of the father or mother.

A parent can give or withhold attention, devastate a child with criticism, or make him happy with a compliment. An awareness of this power puts us as parents in touch with our importance. We learn that authority and power, tempered by timing and restraint in their use, can add to the security of those under their influence. We recognize also that we have the power to undermine our children's sense of security.

The parent role is tiring. At various moments it requires putting aside things we might rather do. It is rewarding, too, bringing us moments of joy and delight. But since those moments may be at times widely spaced, enthusiasm for parenting can be a roller-coaster ride of rising and falling emotions. The effect of this can be most distressing. One source of stability and comfort is the maintenance of an understanding and belief in the importance of the work of being a parent.

Executives, too, have authority and power, which may extend from their jobs into their communities and families. Unlike parenting, the role of executive receives great public admiration as a form of endeavor. The rewards may be more immediate and certainly are often more tangible. Over time, competent executives develop a familiarity with power. Ideally that familarity should evolve into a comfortable and proper use of power through an awareness of the effects it has on others. Thus, as with the parent role, those executives function best who have a sense of their limits and the limits of others.

A capacity for patience and restraint is as necessary to the executive as a capacity for firmness or appropriately aggressive action. The timing of reactions and particular behaviors is key. They make the difference between programs that function well and those that function poorly. (In theme, how similar this is to elements of the parental role!) Enthusiasm and even passion for the role can determine the difference between mediocre results and unusual satisfaction or success. Here, too, an understanding of and a belief in the importance of the particular executive role is essential to maintaining that enthusiasm and an interest in continuity.

Actually, parenting *is* an executive role. (And, in many ways —both symbolic and actual—being an executive is very similar to being a parent; this is seen most obviously in situations of direct supervision.) As said in one book, "Parents today are in some ways like the executives in a large firm—responsible for the smooth coordination of the many people and processes that must work together to produce the final product . . . choosing communities, schools, doctors, and special programs that will leave their children in the best possible hands.''[5] Seen in this context, the role of parent may have an additional attraction for those who are executives by choice.

2

The Executive Career

There are approximately 9.5 million executives in the United States. Seventy-eight percent are males, and 22 percent females. The vast majority (80 percent) work as salaried employees; the remainder are self-employed. As executives, these people are expected to carry exceptional responsibilities and to exercise leadership. This is what they have in common, though the actual work they do covers a wide range of functions. Administrators and managers are considered here under the common rubric of "executive," although we recognize that their roles can differ considerably depending on the specific area of work—whether it is in the private or public sector; the kind of business, science, university, foundation; etc. Even within the same area, dramatic differences may exist in the amount and levels of authority and power and in the potential for creativity between one executive position and another.

13

As a group, executives work an average of forty-seven and a half hours per week, excluding hours spent in local or long-distance travel and time spent in business-related entertainment. Thirty-eight percent of the executives work forty-nine or more hours per week. Twenty-two percent of women executives and 42 percent of male executives work more than forty-nine hours each week.[1]

Given the number of hours worked, time obviously becomes the most precious of resources for such individuals. Because of this reality, a series of questions (often begging for attention and just as often neglected) presents itself to executives.

- How much time should be spent with work and work-related activities?
- How much time should be spent with the family?
- How does one relate family to work?
- How much time can one afford for exercise, for leisure, and for community activities?
- Is it all right, given all these demands, to have a nonstructured leisure, occasionally—to just loaf or wander or sit?

I hope you will consider these questions as you review throughout this book your behaviors as executive and parent. My responses to these questions are presented in the last chapter.

How an individual becomes an executive rather than engaging in some other form of work has received relatively little study. Still, some patterns do emerge. As an occupational choice, the executive role tends to be assumed by those who reveal certain preferred behaviors during their childhood and adolescence. These individuals are likely to be outer-directed, motivated to action, and intense in play and/or work. Many show themselves highly motivated to control events, but they also enjoy working both with and in groups and/or on teams.[2] These characteristics, whether in males or females, usually are clearly seen well before the age of eighteen years. Naturally, such characteristics lead to a variety of adult roles. The final occupational choice of being an executive seems to come about through serendipity combined with the individual's freedom and talent for taking advantage of opportunities as they arise.

A by now venerable definition of executive work describes it as "the specialized work of maintaining an organization and operation . . . maintain [ing] a system of cooperative effort."[3] Assume with me that this definition reasonably describes the role. A little reflection suggests to us the potential executives have for experiencing high levels of stress. One element of executive stress comes from the relatively constant vigilance needed in such work. Generally, the executive is responsible for the maintenance of the flow, structure, and function of an organization; he or she must deal constantly with a great number of events and details while delegating authority to other individuals and drawing from them their best cooperative efforts.

The role is ideally proactive: The executive supplies energy to the system, pushing it forward and always looking ahead rather than simply maintaining a steady state. The daily environment, with its constant demands, drains off energy through a never-ending flow of details and issues "crying for" attention. Judgment is constantly exercised in the setting of priorities. Those individuals in particular who combine a high degree of compulsiveness (attention to details) with a strong sense of responsibility must develop a capacity for "selective irresponsibility" vis-à-vis the unsolicited, excessive demands for attention and action. An executive's world is best described as one of input overload.

Facilitator, overseer, synthesizer, and sometimes builder and creator of new activities, the executive is committed to work of the most intense, preoccupying kind. Executive work can devour energy and time in gargantuan amounts. Unless executives make special efforts at setting limits to their responses to the demands, they risk becoming so involved in their work that they isolate themselves from others. For some executives, years flash by, even a lifetime, without their being much aware of the distance they have put between themselves and such important others as spouse and children. Without empathy, without pity, and without ultimate gratitude (despite salaries and special awards), the system voraciously demands more and more. Those of limited insight become swept up in it and are victimized by it, whereas the aware are simply duped by their own illusions and fantasies of control. Both tumble through the torrent, losing bits of themselves without noticing the loss. The survivors are seen by others for what they have become: individuals who have lost their capacities for responsiveness, sharing, growth, and wonder.

Executives can have their responsibilities and their freedom too. No matter what one's line of endeavor, there is no need to be victimized or controlled by one's career. We all have the responsibility to be self-aware, particularly if we are of normal good fortune and adequate resources. In thinking about our behavior, relationships, and directions in life—barring dramatic ill fortune—none of us should claim to ourselves or to anyone else that we are victims. As Honoré de Balzac says: "L'homme supérieur épouse les événements et les circonstances pour les conduire."

NORMAL CHALLENGES IN EXECUTIVE LIFE

During the course of each executive's life, a series of normal challenges can be expected to occur. Those that relate specifically to work include the assignment of a sudden additional task, demands for increased output and/or quality of performance, a new job or new assignment, moves within the organization, or moves at the organization's request from one community to the other, as well as various kinds of negative actions that a corporate system or other system may impose on an individual (demotions or withholding of advancement). Such challenges obviously can be crises. How significant they are as tests of one's talents and tensile strengths depends on many factors. Events prior to the particular challenge, the state of one's physical and emotional health, and the kind and status of family and other support systems—all have a bearing on how successfully one can deal with a particular challenge.

Challenges originating outside the workplace, usually in the individual's personal life, often affect functioning at work. Examples include marital problems, actual separation or divorce, chronic behavioral problems in children, health problems in oneself or in members of the family, drug or alcohol abuse problems, and serious accidents. Each one of these personal challenges raises concerns not only about self-image but also about family image and the image of oneself within the community.

What has been discussed is applicable to all executives. Yet beyond these, added stresses exist for those executives who belong to the so-called special populations: women, the racial minorities, and the physically handicapped. Members of each group face additional challenges in their executive and family roles, and the dimensions of that added stress need to be acknowledged. Although I treat these special populations together, I realize their separateness and the tremendous differences in the challenges their members face. Nevertheless, women, the racial minorities, and the handicapped are united by more than their need to cope with issues above and beyond those experienced by other executives; they are united also by their sharing of stigma. Easily recognized in the workplace, they are seen in terms of socially programmed preconceptions which influence both the attitudes and behaviors of the people they work with. Because of these preconceptions, co-workers have difficulty relating to the individual as such. As an illustration, simply consider the following life caricatures: women being equated with sexual pleasure, comforting (nurturance), and birthing; the black or Hispanic being equated with poor education, "impoverished" cultural background, a lesser intellectual and moral endowment; and the handicapped person as crippled, an object of pity, less competent than others and basically as a taker rather than a giver. Such caricatures live on. They influence reactions and opportunities; they limit the minority worker's chances for creative functioning and advancement. Worse yet, the stigma and the associated behaviors of others cause various conflicts in the stigmatized. Such individuals find that their roles, their sense of adequacy and inadequacy, and their sense of value to themselves and others are all called into question.

THE WOMAN EXECUTIVE

A woman executive is a woman. At this time in our history, as in the past, she has her own mother as an internalized reference point, and that mother, most likely, was not an executive. Today's woman executive finds herself caught up in the currents of rapid social change, in which the social and economic roles of women are subject to thorough reassessment. The shorthand term for this cultural revolution is "the women's liberation movement." This movement touches everyone in the society, effecting changes in the lives of men, children, and families. The woman executive finds herself somewhere on a spectrum of values being enunciated by various women's groups—the National Organization for Women (NOW) on one end and the Martha Movement on the other. Yet the woman seeking to define her own individuality gets only limited help from the movement. Ultimately, she can define her own individuality only through her own efforts.

"Movements" and their leaders do serve to stimulate dialogue. They also, by exhorting women to respond to new cultural values and activities, send out "siren calls," which can dramatically change the life experiences of individual women. The woman executive who heeds the challenge of the women's movement begins to question much that she had previously accepted, particularly in regard to the cultural activities of her family of origin as well as her family of the moment. Thus, while meeting the stern demands of her executive and family roles, she must also find ways to integrate these external pressures for change in her day-to-day life as a woman. To engage in such integration and the necessary reflection is no mean challenge. It takes energy and often produces a sense of internal discomfort, of tension and uncertainty. Such private struggles in the female executive, apart from any publicly acknowledged success or nonsuccess in her executive role, can lead to anxiety and depression.

Unlike men, most women in our society do not automatically obtain the rewards of community approbation, spouse respect and appreciation, and peer-group support. Indeed, the reality is just the opposite. When executive women are overtly aggressive in their pursuit of excellence and/or success, they quickly become aware of uneasiness, guardedness, and disapproval in others. Women executives are clearly more hard put to find the sources of emotional sustenance that assist *everyone* in life, whether the stresses they deal with are ordinary or great. They are constantly drained of energy by conflicting demands, double messages, and opposing expectations. To cope, they mobilize styles of behavior, "masks," and other defenses. The struggles to mobilize these defenses can produce subclinical depressions that evolve into chronic mood states of dissatisfaction and feelings of isolation. In their attempts to cover these states, women executives not infrequently resort to increased activity or the actual assumption of one of the expected caricature roles, such as the "aggressive, castrating bitch," the "deceptively helpless, manipulative maneuverer," or the "seductive, moody, loyalty-changing climber."

Women who cope successfully with these incredibly challenging stresses do exist. Such women have the ability to remain in touch with themselves, to deal with the system without allowing distortion of their basic values and without making the kinds of accommodation that result in chronic repressed anger. Many such women had special sources of sustenance as they grew: a supportive mother and/or father, an important "other" individual, or a role model in the form of a relative or teacher. Identifying with such figures as one grows provides a basis for the adult's capacity to form warm, supportive relationships with other individuals and with the community and to construct or affiliate himself or herself with a belief system. The combination of these things results in a strength and capacity to cope that enable women executives to grow and develop in a less than optimal adult environment.

Among the less subtle sources of heightened stress on women executives is the reality that if they choose to be executives *and* have husbands and children, they take up a struggle which puts them in the category of "superfemale," "supermomma," and "superwoman." The energy output required of and delivered by such women is extraordinary. They have little time for insight and introspection as they superhumanly switch roles from executive to homemaker (another form of executive), to wife, mother, and lover. Usually, a woman handles this struggle by creating stages in her life (mother stage, work stage—many variations on this theme exist) or by compartmentalizing her activities while relying heavily on housekeepers and relatives to fill in for her at home.

THE MINORITY EXECUTIVE

Blacks, Hispanics, Asians, and Native Americans (American Indians, Aleuts, Eskimos, Native Hawaiians) form the principal racial minorities in the United States. Members of each racial minority must deal with stigma as well as other special stresses. Events in their history as a people influence the forms and intensity of the stigmas that are attached to them. Their history also predetermines what attitudes they as individuals can expect to encounter in their interactions with members of the dominant white culture. All racial minority members in this society are exposed to the mistrust and fear of nonminority people and systems.

When minority individuals become executives, they must contend with pride and loneliness. They become one of a small group amid the many people who surround them. Pride in their position, with its statement about achievement and its socioeconomic potential, is countered by the loneliness they feel in being relatively unusual. They are automatically labeled as different because of their surface appearance, even though they work as hard as their white counterparts, desire the same comfort and status for themselves and their families, and have the same energy levels and intellect.

Always in the background is their group's history and the influence it exerts on the present. History here means both the actual memories and the symbolic meanings of past events—for example, the World War II American internment camps for Japanese-American families, the lynchings of blacks (U.S. Census records of these ceased in 1935), the mob actions against blacks (last major occurrences were in 1955), and the multiple broken agreements and treaties with American Indians. It was only in the 1960s that society began to give increased attention to the civil and moral rights of racial minorities. Government cautioned business to open more and better job opportunities to minority workers, and minority leaders urged members to stop disguising or low-profiling their true identity. Today's minority executives cannot help but have these realities in mind as they relate to others in the greater community, as well as in the workplace.

As minority executives attain privilege and possessions, they often find themselves distanced from many of their minority friends and their families. They feel pride in these achievements, but they also feel guilt. Both majority and minority members may despise them for seeking or allowing themselves to be "co-opted" by the system. These suspicions may be put to them in no uncertain terms. By now classic expressions such as, "He's an Oreo, black on the outside and white on the inside," reflect complex, intense, guilt-engendering feelings.

To cope with their realities, many minority executives work hard at their jobs while intensely pursuing an identity that is "right"—right for the greater society and for the executive position itself. In addition, they tend to exaggerate the compartmentalization we all engage in between work and home by keeping family and real friends as isolated as possible from the workplace. For example, one authority on blacks refers to the work world as the "sustaining environment."[4] That environment, with its predominantly Caucasian values, is intensely production- and time-oriented; it confers power and material resources. On the other hand, the "nurturing environment"—that of language, music, time, and values—exists away from the workplace. Only in the "nurturing environment" can the minority executive truly relax and drop his or her guardedness. Only in the family and home community can he or she feel safe, accepted, and protected. This movement back and forth between sustaining and nurturing environments consumes a great deal of energy and increases the potential for conflict. The executive shuttlecocks between opposing values and differing rewards. The result is increased stress, more than that faced by those who do not come from a minority group.

THE PHYSICALLY HANDICAPPED EXECUTIVE

With handicapped executives, the challenges they have always faced in their own existence are transposed to a world of high expectations and competitiveness. Some of these challenges are mundane (how to get about in a wheelchair, how to get into a bathroom stall), but others, such as stigma and intrusive curiosity, are more difficult to handle. Handicapped people are often caricatured and are often the object of morbid, sometimes frightened interest. They encounter in others a disbelief in their capacities for self-care and an assumption that because they are handicapped they must be unhappy or deserving of pity. Beyond these "ordinary" challenges, energies must be spent on the special arrangements and special activities demanded by their careers. Travel, although possible, needs special attention whether one is considering public transportation, cars, trains, airplanes, or going from one's home to the subway. Further, handicapped individuals must learn to accept help and to ask for it when needed. This must coexist with their insistence on autonomy and the freedom to strive competitively with others. By the time a handicapped individual has reached an executive position, he or she has mastered all these challenges. Nonetheless, maintaining that mastery in an executive role is a source of ongoing stress. As a handicapped individual, one is more sensitive to the subtle challenges that always exist between competitors. In any individual, overresponse to the challenge to prove oneself puts that individual under the control of others and sets the pattern for a never-ending, sometimes frantic pursuit of attainment, which, if not beyond possibility, is certainly beyond reason.

HOW EXECUTIVES COPE

Whatever stresses may be special to certain groups of executives, there are certain responses to stress that tend to be exhibited by executives in every group. In almost all cases, these responses have consequences in the executive's relationships with his or her spouse and children.

Executives of all backgrounds and both sexes tend to become "socialized into their occupational culture."[5] This means that they assume to varying degrees the behavioral repertoire and values promoted by their occupation. By taking on the behaviors and values associated with one's work, a person modifies his or her responses to stress, even to the point of being unaware that his or her behavior is a reaction to stress. An all too common example involves the male or female executive who progresses from nonuse or occasional use of alcohol to alcoholism.[6] The transition into excessive use of or addiction to alcohol often occurs insidiously, without the person being aware of the change. Social drinking at business lunches and at business-related evening entertainment is part of the occupational culture. Even when the behavior is called to the executive's attention, he or she, while acknowledging that indeed these changes are occurring, is often bewildered as to the reason for them.

We all have our own unique responses to our reality, which includes work-related pressures. One way of understanding these differences is to think about each one of us having our own special set of "lenses" through which we see the world. What we see through these lenses greatly influences our particular responses to stress. These metaphorical lenses were ground by our early life experiences out of the material of our individual temperaments (genetically determined reactivity to internal and external stimuli) and were colored by our ethnic, subcultural, and family background.

To understand how this process works, consider Mr. X as he surveys the task of reorganizing a new division: Despite all the thoughtful, careful planning he has already done, he still has not covered all contingencies. He sees reality in such a way that unless he has covered all possible contingencies, the performance of the task is not acceptable to him. The performance demands this executive makes on himself become a major source of inner tension and chronic stress: He never can account for *all* contingencies. If things do not work out for him, guilt, anger, and extreme self-blame are his lot.

Mr. Y, reviewing the same reorganization of a new division with different lenses yet with the same level of experience, sees that he has carried out a thoughtful, careful planning job. He realizes that unexpected complications or interferences might arise. This realization summarizes his contingency planning. He knows that if unpredicted events occur to complicate or interfere with his task, somehow he will handle the situation. Mr. Y's experience of tension and stress, as well as his vulnerability to guilt and anger around this task, are considerably less than Mr. X's.

When executives fail to cope well with stress, the fallout appears in work and in private life. Alcoholism has already been mentioned. It has tragically signed the death warrant of many brilliant executive careers. Whether the apparent cause is alcoholism or something else, poor functioning in response to stress causes the executive to lose work efficiency and sharpness of thinking and to suffer from impaired judgment. Creativity evaporates while she or he struggles simply to maintain the status quo. Extension of poor functioning into family life is the rule rather than the exception. Indeed, sometimes the first signs of dysfunction at work are evidenced at home. Communication with spouse and children degenerates. Withdrawal or various forms of acting out occur, sometimes seen as loss of perspective and of impulse control. Resultant behaviors may be any of the following: sexual affairs, spouse (most commonly wife) abuse,[7] drug abuse, excessive unnecessary traveling, and various physical complaints accompanied by hypochondriacal behavior. The multiple stresses in their lives make executives highly vulnerable to all these dysfunctions. For them, for their families, and for their organizations, their ability to cope with stress, as a fundamental process, takes on critical dimensions, and thus conscious efforts must be made to enhance coping skills.

FOUR SOURCES OF STRENGTH

Many ways exist for coping with stress; no single style or approach serves everyone. The most successful coping styles take into account at least four major realities in the lives of the individuals who cope: their knowledge of themselves, the existence and quality of their intimate relationships with others, the family and subculture they come from, and the communities (work and outside work) in which they reside.

We all cope best if our resources are intact. These resources include health, intellect, positive past experiences in dealing with stress, internalized beliefs and values, and material comfort. A lessening or significant loss in any of these areas immediately lowers a person's ability to cope. And sometimes situations occur in which multiple stresses exist simultaneously (financial strain, poor health, loss of a loved one).

Elements needed for successful coping exist within the individual, in the couple (if the individual is married), in the family, and in the community. Such elements are numerous and interact in multiple complex ways. Underlying them all is our belief in the power we have to exercise control in our lives and some control over life events.

Individuals draw first on their own psychology and intellect. Various psychological processes, called defense mechanisms, may be mobilized in response to different challenging situations. The most obvious such response is "trying to think things out," known in psychiatric lingo as *intellectualization*. All executives use it when things don't go as they should; they spend time trying to figure out what went wrong and how to bring about the desired change. If this fails, they may *rationalize* that failure, telling themselves and their colleagues that the goal was not so important anyway or that it was only a trial or putting in its place some alternative to which they suddenly attach more importance.

Another psychological coping device involves redirecting our energies; we turn away from something that did not work out and become intensely involved in other activities in order to keep our mind off the problem. Thus, many psychological defenses are two-edged swords. These include denial—becoming consciously unaware that undesired things are happening—and repression—forcing oneself to forget something or putting it out of one's mind.

Psychological defenses can even result in physical changes. An individual who does not feel stressed may develop a physiological problem expressed through such symptoms as headaches, diarrhea, or ulcers. The protection from conscious awareness of chronic stress is paid for by the body, which experiences the stress in terms of physiological imbalances; the particular manifestation is determined by one's genetic makeup and early life experiences. This defense mechanism is labeled *somatization*. It is considered, obviously, a maladaptive way of coping. Other maladaptive ways of coping include excesses in drinking, smoking, or substance abuse.

In our culture, ideal coping means taking some positive action on the basis of as much understanding of a situation as possible. Avoiding the issues, or driving them underground beneath the level of conscious awareness, is not a satisfactory way to cope. What resources, then, do we all have?

The vast array of coping resources begins with ourselves, particularly what we learn from past experiences. Our cultural approach to problem solving is to try to figure out why and how things are going wrong. The next level of sophistication in this self-evaluation process includes thinking about "why" and "how" with reference to our successes, too. Whether we are considering an interaction with an individual, a complex business transaction, or a family problem, we automatically strive to improve on things. We use resources beyond ourselves by talking things over with a spouse or friend or seeking counsel from an authority figure (a parent, former teacher, or clergyperson). In certain kinds of situations we go to a healer for short-term assistance (included here would be individual and group therapy). The environment also helps us to cope. Consider how easily we can change and vary our immediate surroundings and how many different ways there are of enjoying them, such as going on a walk, a hike, a trip or just withdrawing into a comfortable, familiar place.

Within a social system such as ours, in which monogamous relationships are promoted, the couple can provide psychological support for either partner. How much assistance and refuge it offers depends on the couple's history; the members' original "contract" about expectations, obligations, and performance with each other; and basic trust and mutual respect they have evolved for each other over time. When all these elements are favorable, the couple relationship becomes a tremendous source of sustenance to a member under stress.

Similarly, the family can be a major buffer and support in times of acute and chronic stress. It serves as a secure refuge where emotions may be safely vented. It is a source of advice, and by raising other issues, it inadvertently helps to keep the problems of the workplace in perspective. Here again, the family's history, with the degrees of basic trust and mutual respect developed over time, determines how available and useful it will be to the individual member who is trying to cope with stress.

The community is another potential element in any coping system, and, indeed, it should be. The community's traditions and values are solid reference points which help to comfort and explain. Participation in a community, as in the family, also extends an individual's identity beyond the workplace. Without this participation, an executive is in danger of assigning exclusive and overwhelming importance to work or work-associated events.

Executives have the same external support systems available to everyone: the family in its various forms, friends, churches, clubs, and community activities. Beyond these, what resources do executives have for coping with stress and what strategies can they utilize to enhance that coping? Executives have specifically job-related supports that usually are not available to all members of our society. These include a better-than-average income;[8] special health and recreational benefits; professional networks; and special supports such as staff assistants, executive secretaries, and secretarial pools. These latter individuals are there precisely to help the executive get things done. They serve the executive as important but often unrecognized buffers against excessive and undesired input.

STRATEGIES FOR BETTER COPING

To be even more specific about ways of coping, I recommend the following six strategies to executives under stress from family or work-related demands:

1. Review your personal resources to determine if they are intact or if they need improvement. If demands you once handled easily now loom large, it may simply be the result of a health problem or, as is common, excessive fatigue. The first line of approach, then, is to take steps to remedy this situation— to get medical advice or to take time out for rest. If financial resources are your problem, no matter what the overt cause is, a review and perhaps some outside counseling are necessary. •

2. Make a carefully reasoned admission to yourself that things are not going well. This statement must be followed up by observing , questioning, information gathering, and differentiating the certain from the not so certain. Such an approach turned on one's self is no different from what a competent executive does when problem solving on the job.

3. Review all the possible outcomes of the problematical situation and imagine to yourself exactly how you would feel about and deal with each of the likely possibilities. This process, a

type of "cognitive rehearsal," helps us to anticipate change. Because of their unexpectedness, extent, or particular nature, changes sometimes cause heightened stress; we feel overwhelmed or not in control. When we anticipate changes, however, their power to distress us is diminished.

4. Accept the reality that changes produce stress and that stress cannot exist without change. Moreover, accept that both conditions exist in all lives forever. This acceptance provides a solid foundation for our efforts to cope as challenge succeeds challenge in the course of our working lives.

5. Understand that your body works powerfully for you in your efforts to cope. During times of stress our bodies respond with heightened alertness and inner tension. These reactions are designed to ensure our survival. They supply increased aggressiveness and a capacity to fight or struggle beyond ordinary levels or, if necessary, to flee from whatever threatens us. These feelings and energies become our allies as we strive to maintain control.

6. Since each of us copes differently, it is wise not to try to impose our styles on others or, without reflection, to assume their styles for our own. Also, coping styles vary at different ages and developmental stages. The approaches to dealing with problem situations on the work or home front that proved useful in one's twenties may not serve so well in one's thirties, and those developed in the thirties may not serve so well in the forties or fifties. In all situations of stress, regardless of their source, those who cope best realize their individuality and are able to relate in some way to both the community and the family.

A NEW PHILOSOPHY OF WORK

Earlier I described some executives as being so caught up in their system that they are tumbled by the torrent of the system's demands. Family and workplace compete for their energies—physical, emotional, and intellectual. This conflict leads to the "head-heart dichotomy" (as it is termed by Michael Maccoby in his book *The Gamesman*) that is so familiar to executive parents. The phenomenon raises some important questions. How can an individual avoid being thus swept away? Where and how does one find the solid handholds and reference points? Are individuals who perform executive functions prisoners of necessity of their occupations?

Sufficient time and energy does exist for family, for parenting, and for work. Human energies, attention span, flexibility, and tensile strength are all highly expansible. We all have within us many untapped resources. Parental behaviors are dramatically influenced by our individual needs at the moment, our moods, and our health and levels of fatigue. Work obviously plays a major role here, as illustrated in the following sketches:

Sketch 1

Smiling, full of energy, mischief, and affection, Jenny, age five years, joyfully skips to her father as he comes through the door. She is delighted to see him and eager to show her day's accomplishments—some crayon drawings and a newly scraped knee covered with a real bandage.

RESPONSE 1. Tense, tired from work, her father feels his fatigue lift before her enthusiasm, her joy, and her energy. Thoughts of work seem to leave his mind as he picks up and hugs his already chattering daughter.

RESPONSE 2. Tense, tired from work, her father is irritated by her energetic, joyful approach. He feels as if it is an assault on him. This particular day at work has not made him feel good about himself. He needs to be alone for a bit; he really has to be quiet, maybe have a drink, unwind, and chat with his wife without the children.

Sketch 2

Johnny's father has a lot of work to do that night in preparation for an important conference the next day. Yet even before dinner is finished, Johnny's asthmatic attack has gotten worse despite giving the prescribed medications. His nostrils are flaring, his chest heaving; Johnny obviously needs a trip to the hospital emergency room.

RESPONSE 1. Mary has to stay with the baby—can't get a sitter on such short notice. Damn it to hell, why does that little bastard always seem to get one of these attacks when it really screws up everyone's schedule. I might be at the hospital all night with him. This just happens too many times.

RESPONSE 2. Mary has to stay with the baby—Johnny needs one of us with him. Johnny really looks terrified just like he does every time he has a bad asthmatic attack. Poor little guy, I guess he may be at the hospital all night. I can take my papers and sit next to him and work when he is no longer so panicked or is sleeping.

The different behaviors by apparently different parents could just as well be given by the same parent depending upon their needs of the moment, moods, fatigue, and health. Related to these factors are others: the individual parent's personality, their feelings about parenting and about family, and their interactions with their spouses.

Thirty-nine years ago two students of work in the United States wrote:

> The work a man does to earn his livelihood stamps him with mental and physical traits characteristic of the form and level of his labor, defines his circle of friends and acquaintances, affects the use of his leisure, . . . limits his interests and attainment of his aspirations and tends to set the boundaries of his culture.[9]

These observations are in general as accurate today as in 1940 when they were made, despite four decades of social and technological change that have made our present-day culture the most self-conscious, self-observing, and self-questioning in Western history. Yet until recently, executives have remained relatively aloof from this evolution. As a group, they have been largely deaf to the questions raised by the issues concerning one's personal reference points and values.

This situation has begun to change, however. Executives, particularly because of the challenges and stresses of their work and the systems within which they work, realize that they must develop their capacities to reflect on their existence and on their culture, to see meaning and importance in things beyond themselves and their work. This they can do through religious and philosophical reference points within family groups and friend networks. Out of this effort comes a greater awareness of the effects their power, influence, and material resources (no matter at what level they were) have on others. This move toward reflection on values helps them discover the needed handholds within family, friends, church, and community and saves them from losing perspective, indeed from losing their "selves." More and more executives are seeking reference points beyond their work. The legend of King Midas is as much a parable on values as on greed.

3

To Be a Parent

We all tend to use words without stopping to reflect on their original meaning. If you check a dictionary about the frequently used word *parent,* you will see that its original meaning refers simply to the act of creating or generating another of one's kind.[1] Only derivative meanings speak of the more elaborate process of nurturing a child with physical care, emotional support, and education. That process of nurturing goes on all around us; it is a familiar behavior of adult mammals and many nonmammals. This may be stating the obvious, but remember that *obvious* and *familiar* do not equate with *simple.* By really looking at familiar things, by reexamining them rather than always taking them for granted, we can obtain important insights into our lives as individuals and as members of the human community.

Today, for all of us, it is critical to reexamine what it means to be a parent. The increased complexity of our world, generated by rapid technological development, dramatic social change, and vastly expanded information exchange, has enlarged our opportunities and has multiplied our stresses. As with many aspects of life, raising a family today is a very different proposition from what it was for earlier generations. Parents are still responsible for the physical protection, nutrition, emotional support, and the setting of limits for their children; these behaviors serve to organize reality for the parents themselves and for their children. But in today's world these responsibilities involve complex issues. For example, should you, as a parent, be concerned about cholesterol, sugars, and nitrites and other food additives? What kind of concern and how much would be appropriate? Should you as a mother breast- or bottle-feed your infant? What flame-retardant pajamas are safe? How early should your child attend school? What are your responsibilities concerning influences from outside the family, be they from other children, other people, or the media? The number of such issues could run on for pages. No wonder books and pamphlets about parenting are so popular. No wonder that we parents look for formulas to guide us in the process of being a parent. No wonder that we often have an unmet need for reassurance about the job we are doing as parents.

In trying to do the best for their children, today's parents are prey to self-consciousness and tension. They scrutinize their nurturing instincts, feelings, behaviors to the extent that the richness and joys of being a parent are often dampened, even obscured. This should not be so. Parenting is not only the most important contribution parents can make to their society and species during their lives but also the most challenging, fascinating, and rewarding of roles. I would like you to experience it as such as you explore with me this familiar terrain. Two areas deserve particular attention. The first of these concerns the factors that affect your experience of parenting and your capacity to be a parent, and these are discussed in this chapter. The second concerns the question of how one functions as a parent. The latter concern is the subject of chapter 4.

THE PARENT AS A PERSON

What you are like as a person is the first among many factors that determine how you act in the parent role. Are you tense, hard-driving, and single-minded? Are you able to vary your behavior with different situations, able to move from being guarded, intense, goal-directed to being open, relaxed, comfortable with the flow of events? How much knowledge of yourself —your needs, your strengths, and your limitations—do you have? How comfortable and happy are you with yourself as a person? Do you like other people and find pleasure in listening to them, observing them, and responding to them? The answers you give to these questions will depend very much on certain realities in your life, including your past experience (particularly your own childhood), your current needs, your socioeconomic status, your health, and your beliefs and values. All these profoundly influence you as a person, affecting both how you function as a parent and how you feel about the role.

Ghosts do exist. They leave their traces on every day of our lives—if by ghosts we are understood to mean those past experiences that affect present behavior and feelings. Many ghosts, good and bad, arise when we play the role of parent. Each of us can find memories of our experiences in our actions and responses as parents. We comfort our children as we remember times in childhood when we felt frightened, hurt, and with no control or out of control. We relate easily with them as we recall times of play, of dreaming, and of special adventures with friends. (An inability to recall such times—perhaps for lack of such experiences—sets the stage for aloofness from one's children, even a resentful misunderstanding of them.) We should be able—even if it takes some effort—to recall the feelings we had while playing games at home and at school: the intensity and occasional tension and our irritability at having to learn control. Our own struggles to be "grown up" should be memories we can call upon. Do we remember how grown-ups appeared to us? Were they fearsome, unpredictable, and powerful creatures (the "monsters" of the two- to five-year-olds)? Were they comforting, tender, strong, free, and bigger people we wanted to be like? Were they some combination of both? We should try to replay in our minds our childhood friendships and group activities—the enthusiasms we shared with other kids, for moths or baseball cards or reading or whatever. All these experiences of the past contributed to making you the person you are today. They also predisposed you to certain behaviors as a parent.

A fund of these events, in which the child experiences his or

her own capabilities, contributes significantly to the child's becoming an adult who feels secure, in control of himself or herself and of most life events. Without them, the child may grow
into an adult who lacks such feelings. The difference largely
explains why some adults are capable of regularly responding,
cuddling, playing, feeling, and being relaxed with a child and
why others are either incapable of such behaviors or perform
them erratically and as much in response to their own needs as
those of the child.

In childhood we all learned about things that were outside of
us and things that were inside us, and we learned that these
things could make us feel and react in different ways. Among
these things were information and ideas: We learned that we
could give them out as well as receive them. We learned about
feelings, too—how to name them, express them, and control
them. We learned how to modify our various reactions and
behaviors. Those of us who did not learn such things as children
often have difficulty later functioning in our roles as adults and
parents. Those of us who grew up with impulsive, abusive
adults and parents (or parent figures) who controlled neither
their feelings nor their aggressive behaviors have a high potential for repeating such behaviors when we become parents with
children of our own.

Past experience combined with immediate realities determines our current personal needs. What these needs are, and
how they are met, obviously influences parental behavior. Such
needs are physical and emotional. They include rest (fatigue
tends to reduce our control over impulsive behaviors and private thoughts), time alone and time away from child-care responsibilities, feeling loved and respected, and having access to
the intellectual and social stimulation of other adults. Part of the
self-inventory that all of us should do periodically must be a
review of these needs and whether or not they are being met. If
they are not, we should take what action we can to correct the
situation. When basic needs are neglected, our capacities for
empathy, spontaneity, humor, and pleasure decrease. As a con-
sequence, emotional tensile strength is lost, reducing our coping
capacities and hence our abilities to handle the work of
parenting.

PARENTS GROW TOO

Being a parent fulfills a variety of psychological and social needs. It adds something to us as individuals. For example, as fathers and mothers we learn a lot about ourselves through a variety of processes. One is mimicry: Children incorporate, often quite literally, the nonverbal and verbal behaviors of their parents. There will be echoes of yourself and/or your spouse in the authoritarian or bossy way your child speaks when scolding another, in the turns of phrase and facial expressions your offspring use (particularly the three- to six-year-olds), and in their body language—the way they move, how they hold themselves while resting, looking, or exclaiming. When we as parents notice these behaviors and recognize them as deriving from us, our often surprised recognition can have the same kind of powerful effects on self-awareness that videotape playbacks have when used in individual and family therapy settings. Such behaviors by children reflect parental attitudes that often are worth examining. They can help us come to a better understanding of our needs and behaviors as human beings. Further self-knowledge is gleaned from our reactions to the various challenging situations that children present to us. We are called on to control our impulses (not to push away, hit, withdraw, scream, fondle), to put off immediate gratification (such as a play or movie, a hot shower or bath, a walk), and to remember always that we are different from our children and that they are different from us. Our successes and our failures in these efforts teach us a lot about ourselves.

We fathers have the same general vocabulary of needs as do mothers. And potentially we can receive from the parental role many of the same gratifications it provides to mothers. Unfortunately, our culture, until recently, promoted the detachment of fathers from the parental role. This distancing lessened the contribution that fathers made to family life. It also deprived them of having various needs met and of attaining the kind of insights and self-knowledge we have just discussed. Both the children and their parents lose when fathers are not involved. Fathers may try to recapture what is lost by joining in organized activities. Or they may wait until their children are in their late teens and then try to "talk to them." But after years of nonintimacy, coming close to their children proves a most elusive goal. Indeed, in middle age, many men realize that they have lost a precious opportunity, that their needs have not and never will be met. Some try desperately to establish a parent-child relationship with their teenage or young adult child. Almost always the result is bitter disappointment for all concerned. Often only regret remains: "I have neither the time now nor the strength to embark upon a voyage of exploration with the object of finding the reality of others."[2]

CONSUMERISM AND PARENTS

Intense are the external pressures put on all of us to consume and to possess. These pressures testify to the great importance that socioeconomic status has in our society. One is made to feel less in control, perhaps even less "whole," if he or she hasn't the resources to attain those things that are presented for consumption.

In such an environment the level and stability of one's income gets much attention. When as parents our ability to provide resources is unstable or marginal, we are uncomfortable, even chronically tense and irritable. Feelings of inadequacy and even anger develop; the sales messages bombard us daily from all forms of the media. Unfortunately, in our society the self-image of adults is very much tied in with their capacity to attain material goods. For many individuals who are heavily influenced by the ethos of consumerism and by the media siren calls to buy this or fly there, economic uncertainty results in withdrawal from the family, even dysfunction. Analyses by such social scientists as Harvey Brenner reveal strong associations between alcoholism, institutionalization for mental illness, and the extreme uncertainty experienced during unemployment.[3]

We do not have to be such prisoners of our culture. To pretend these pressures do not exist or that they are not powerful is not what I suggest. Rather, we can make unceasing efforts to define those things that are truly necessary and important to us and to our children. These efforts we make toward self-definition, assessment of personal needs, and reflection on one's values are the first steps in freeing oneself from what is for many the tyranny of materialism and of consumerism. If done effectively, they make an important contribution to the education of one's children and the protection of one's family.

HEALTH: PHYSICAL AND MENTAL

Our physical health influences our functioning in all realms. Its effects on parenting can be particularly dramatic. Naturally, if we are robust, strong parents, the physical and even emotional resources available to us are greater than if energies are drained by frailty or frank ill health. When acutely or chronically ill, we become preoccupied with ourselves—with our physical selves, our reduced social functioning, the stability of our income status, our interactions with family members, and our future return to "normal" functioning. Our basic human need to feel whole, to feel "in control" is not being met at such times. Thus, situations of poor or frank ill health or of serious injury always reduce our psychological tensile strength; we usually become more irritable, less empathetic, less flexible, less in control of our impulses, and more in need of being nurtured and hence less able to nurture.

It is important to be aware of the effects disabilities have on our functioning. Awareness allows more deliberate mobilization of personal, family, and community resources to help us meet our continuing needs. Many people meet these challenges in extraordinary fashion. They function with great equanimity and talent in the role of parent even in the face of dramatic personal disability or illness.

SPIRITUAL SUPPORTS

Belief systems are culturally held understandings of life and its predictability. A belief system provides the individual who embraces it with a sense of boundaries and a sense of potential for control over his or her existence. Often, but not necessarily, conveyed through the vehicle of religious beliefs, belief systems provide organizing principles for the daily predictable events of life, as well as the unpredictable events, good or bad.

Values are more a matter of individual concern. Values are the things a person articulates as being desirable, important, and worthwhile to him or her. Values may shift, based on one's culture, one's status in it, one's age and responsibilities, one's work, and whether one has or has not the responsibilities of being a parent.

Belief systems and values provide various organizing principles and reference points which help us to deal with our existences. They help to define ourselves as persons, and they affect how comfortably and well we perform in the parent role. Thus, they influence the current functioning of the family and the future functioning of our children.

Being without values and without belief systems means that one has not defined oneself. One cannot meet the responsibilities of the adult role, much less of the parent role, without such definition. (This, of course, still allows for changes in beliefs and values over time.) The intellectual and psychological framework of beliefs and values determines what we pay attention to, when and what we enjoy, what we dedicate our energies to, what we remember, and what we believe. It is the basis for all our actions and experiences. If our beliefs and values leave little or no room for children and the family, it is questionable whether one should assume the role of parent at all.

The individual parent usually recognizes the importance of being attached to having and caring for children. Indeed, there is in our society (as in most societies) a very real status associated with the parent role. Nevertheless, many adults tend to ignore the importance of that role to the social system. They miss the obvious reality that children and adolescents are part of the human social continuum. On becoming adults, they will either manage, contribute to, or drain from their society. In our old age we become their potential victims if we have allowed them to form hostile or indifferent attitudes about aging and the old. They, the children, procreate the future generations and in turn become parents and teachers. The games, the interrelationships, the studies, and the chores that children engage in while still "little people" or adolescents—all rehearse them for adult performance. Major deprivations—be they spiritual, intellectual, nutritional, or material—distort this rehearsal process, and the distortions are perpetuated into adult life, often taking the form of poor functioning or frank dysfunction in adulthood.

Only when seen in this future perspective, do the real dimensions and importance of parenting become clear. The challenges of the role 'are never ending and difficult. Even those parents who gladly assume the role may have conflicting feelings about it on any one day. Yet even when they are fatigued or feeling cynical, there exists in such parents an undercurrent of satisfaction about their children that they would not have if there weren't considerable rewards in the role.

THE CHILD

Our children influence how we function as parents in ways that cannot be appreciated fully, no matter how much we read or talk about the parent-child relationship. For twenty-four hours a day, for seven days a week, as we are responsible for the nurturance and socialization of another human being, we experience the ebb and flow of intense personal interaction; and in the process we discover previously unidentified resources within ourselves. From fetal life onward, each child affects the life of the parents as individuals and their interactions with important other adults. At each developmental stage of the child—whether *in utero*, infancy, toddlerhood, early childhood, or in the free-roaming, challenging stage called adolescence—the child's needs continue to change. The art and experience of parenting involve meeting those needs even when they are expressed as protests from that very individual, the child, toward whom one is pouring attention and energy.

The influence of the child really begins before conception. Here I speak of the parents' attitude toward having a child. A wished-for child enters a world where his or her parents, because of their desire for him or her, have been preparing themselves to manage and enjoy their role. Such parents are potentially more flexible and adaptable to the demands of child rearing, no matter what demands the child's behavior and existence might impose. The unplanned-for or, even less favorably, the unwanted child enters a world less willing to accommodate and less accepting; the changes that an infant imposes on the parents are poorly received.

As the child's physical presence makes itself felt during his or her prenatal life, parents have an opportunity to begin the process of accommodating to the various changes that child will bring into their lives. Most pregnancies which lead to full-term births proceed smoothly. But where the mother has excessive discomfort or more serious problems such as dramatic morning sickness, first- or second-trimester bleeding requiring bedrest, excessively rapid weight gain, and high blood pressure, the lives of the parents are dramatically changed. They may have feelings of anxiety, tension, guardedness, and sometimes fear about the unborn child. A pregnancy of this sort, however, need not have seriously negative effects on the parent role if the feelings associated with it are recognized and if the outcome of the pregnancy is positive. An infant born prematurely or with a low birth weight presents additional challenges to the parents from the beginning. Often, before such infants can return home, they must remain for several weeks in the hospital. Only recently have obstetricians, pediatricians, and hospitals themselves documented the importance of keeping the mother and father involved with a premature infant during the infant's stay in the hospital. Without such involvement, the emotional feelings of closeness to the child develop less rapidly and less solidly.

Ideally, in problem-free births the mother and father should be in intimate contact with the newborn from the infant's entry into the world. Much recent research has shown the more favorable reactions parents have to the infant and to their new responsibilities when such close and instant contact is encouraged.

Children come into the world as quite complicated creatures. We now have evidence that even *in utero* children respond to sound and light and to the rhythm of different kinds of music, at least during the last three months of pregnancy. After birth, infants can see, and they respond to the rhythm of human voices by moving their bodies in synchrony with such voices; they can smell and respond to gentle holding. Within the first seven to ten days of life, they have evolved into much more complicated creatures than is generally recognized. They are able, for example, to respond differently to different care-givers and to influence the behavior of those persons.[4]

Every infant is different. It comes into this world with its own unique receptivities and reactivities to both internal and external events. It has its own rhythms, its own unique styles of responsiveness. These differences together are called "temperament."[5] They give each infant an individuality which immediately interacts with the individualities of mother, father, or other care-givers, thereby initiating the lifelong interaction that parent and child will have with each other. This individuality is a powerful influencing factor. It is the precursor to the various natural capacities people have for attending or focusing attention, for listening, and for interacting.

People always recognize these early differences, though they rarely consider the implications they have for the future. They may remark, "Isn't he a lively one," "Look at the fight in her," "Isn't she beautiful and cuddly," or "Isn't he powerful and handsome." Such comments are the combinations of the adults' reactions to the infants and the adults' projections of their interpretations of these reactions onto the infant. The reactions that newborns elicit in adults set patterns that can continue for each particular child throughout his or her life. Nursery attendants are very quick to point out the happy babies, the quiet babies, and the exciting babies. The ones classified as happier, healthier babies from the moment they enter the nursery are picked up more, cooed to and talked to more, and, in short, are stimulated more.

What of the situation when the temperament of the child differs from the expectations and needs of the mother? A mother may have wanted or expected a quiet baby of regular rhythms and find herself with a vigorous, loudly protesting infant who has regularly irregular hours. Without some assistance and explanation, such a mother will have great difficulty in attaching herself to the child. Indeed, she may even withdraw from what she sees as an unexpected and overwhelming situation. The opposite sketch also can be drawn: The mother may have expected and wanted a vigorous, protesting child and in reality be confronted with a quiet, regular infant. Her reaction may then be one of disappointment at the child and even concern as to whether it is damaged in some way. Whenever there is a reaction such as the two just described, the groundwork is laid for interferences in parent-child relationships which will evolve until the parents question why things are not quite "right" or until wise and experienced others—a relative or a professional sensitive to such problems—intervenes.

As the child and parent grow, their interactions become modified with life experiences. The interactions do not fundamentally change unless major interventions occur. Children are extensions of the self-image of parents. When the child, even as an infant, is seen as not in synchrony with the parents' expectations and self-image, the potential for unfavorable interactions increases.

The self-images of parents and children are blended not only psychologically but also physically. Any physical or mental defect in a child is unconsciously—and not infrequently even consciously—perceived by the parents as a defect in themselves. If an infant is born with a birth defect, even a mild one, parents seek reasons for this, often searching for some way to assign the blame, fault, and responsibility for this disappointment. An infant born with a cleft lip or palate, even if that infant has no other defects, naturally upsets the parents. Fortunately, today surgical repairs can be performed on many of these minor birth defects within the first two weeks of life and with dramatic success. I believe it is important to remember that any birth defect or birth trauma, no matter how mild, produces an initial psychological "set" in parents toward the child; they henceforth view him or her as having special vulnerabilities. This mental set or attitude differs from that held toward a vigorous, physically whole infant, and again unless there is special reflection and intervention, the stage is set for less than optimal or even unfortunate interactions in the parent-child relationship. As stated earlier, even within the newborn nursery the adult social system begins to act, depending on the physical appearance and behavior of infants. Nurses, attendants, and doctors pick out and play more with the most attractive babies, giving only necessary care to the less attractive ones. Such patterns are perpetuated throughout a child's life and at times evolve into predictable patterns of behavior that he or she will experience within the family and the community.

Developmental stages of children influence the parental role in a variety of ways. Most obvious is that the behaviors of children and their needs differ according to whether they are infants or toddlers, preschoolers or teenagers. At each of these stages the behaviors and needs set different series of interactions with the parents. In addition, different parents, depending on other demands on them in their lives and on their own development as individuals, have varying capacities for coping with the needs of children in their different developmental stages. Unfortunately, relatively few parents are able to observe their own reactions to their children and to develop from these reactions and interactions further insights concerning their behavior as parents.

During infancy, the quality of the infant's interaction with its mother and father lays the groundwork for the infant's comfort with and receptivity to the outside environment. In infancy, the child establishes early body and social rhythms as well as speech and other forms of motor control. The basic foundations for a sense of competence and trust in others occur during the first twelve months of life, and these qualities can evolve at an almost explosive pace during the toddler and preschool period with the acquisition of comfortable motor and language abilities. The first three years of life are critical also for the child's development of social identity as a male or female.

The early school years are important for the acquisition of basic social skills and the related feelings of competence in mastering these skills. The capacity to focus attention and shut out other stimuli in response to personal desires or outside instructions becomes part and parcel of the acquired learning skills of this period. In our current society the school experience can begin as early as two years of age. Thus, beginning at a very tender age the influence of parents and family over child development is no longer exclusive. With the child's entry into school, the power of parents and home begins to wane. Other ideas and behaviors are introduced to children. At first this most powerfully occurs through other children and is largely expressed by mimicry. It is indeed the rare parent who hasn't wondered with great distress where little Johnny or little Isabel picked up a certain style of speech, a certain word, or a certain gesture. As the school years progress, peers become increasingly powerful. Added on to peer influence is that of teachers, including the electronic teacher called television.

This relatively automatic sharing of social responsibilities for children through day-care centers and school systems gradually erodes the influence parents have with their children. Indeed, outside influences are so strong that all of us as parents find ourselves in situations where we must make emphatic efforts to counteract in our children certain behaviors or other developments of which we may not approve. We find, furthermore, that we are drawn to become active in the school and community as one way of having some modifying influence over the actions of these major extrafamilial socializing agents. They have the power to mold the basic temperaments of our children as much as we do within the family; they influence what a child learns and even the child's desire to explore and enjoy.

The period from prepuberty through early adolescence has received much less attention than it warrants, since children have not until recently been seen as particularly troublesome during this stage. Indeed, the neglect is all the greater because the years just before and during early puberty are especially challenging. They are times of active physical changes accompanied by experimentation in social roles beyond the family unit and increased competence in the extrafamilial sphere.

The physical changes of the period are great and most noticeable in the early years. The transition from "ugly duckling" to new self produces clear results, such as increased motor and intellectual competence. In coping with the changes in body image and in learning control over chemically (hormonally) produced moods and reactions to inside and outside stimuli, adolescents learn on their own to deal with stress in a fashion that cannot be taught by others. This learning enriches the psychological self. Finally, adolescence marks experimentation with sexuality and sexual roles in adult society. All these developments and changes are continuing issues we must expect to encounter in our role as parents.

THE FAMILY

We all realize that the family is the basic human social unit. The literature on the subject of families and children is vast and continues to grow. Yet no one has cornered the market on wisdom in this area. No one should be seen as more than a helpful guide and possibly a sensitive teacher.

In its broadest definition, the family is any group of persons with a legal or biologic relationship.[6] It can be defined more narrowly as the "most instinctive fundamental social or mating group in man and animal, especially the union of man and woman through marriage and their offspring; parents and their children."[7]

Recognizing full well that a sophisticated examination of the family in our society requires the broadest definition, I nonetheless encourage here a more focused discussion in which the family is treated as the fundamental social unit for nurturing, training in cultural mores, and structuring the child.[8] Usually the family begins through a ceremonial and legal process in which two opposite-sexed individuals from different biologic lines join to create a new, economic, mating, and social unit— the couple.

"Coupling" is a challenge for some individuals. It certainly is for those who undertake this state of social existence with any degree of commitment and any intent to maintain that relationship over time. Most individuals marry with that intent, yet despite the large amount of available and "recycled" information on marriage and the frequency of dissolved marriages in today's United States, few couples seem aware of the need to work on the maintenance and growth of the unit they have joined to create. It takes work to develop a reciprocal relationship based on mutual understanding, trust, and respect. Indeed, it takes work of the most thoughtful kind to arrive at these points of development.

A variety of things influence the probable outcome of any new marriage. The developmental stage, not necessarily chronological age, of each spouse is one of these things. By developmental stage I am referring to an individual's sense of separation from his or her family, comfort with his or her own autonomy, and sense of security in whatever social role he or she maintains. Related to developmental stages is the degree of self-knowledge that each spouse has attained. Being aware of one's fantasies and desires and being able to express and regulate them color one's interactions with others and the way one manages under stress. The past, too, is important. The childhood experiences of each spouse—the parent-child interactions (caring, sharing, compromising, and cooperating) and the other nurturant experiences (traditions, problems, and conflicts and the handling of these as well as their resolution)—help determine how each member of the couple will react to life experiences and interact with others. Finally, good fortune—the right things happening at the right time or at least a minimum of unfortunate events—is a significant variable.

Major deficits or serious deprivations in any of the above increase the vulnerability of the couple. This is borne out by studies such as that by Theodore Lidz and his colleagues, which reveals that "the couples' difficulties in gaining reciprocal relationships and mutual satisfaction arose more commonly from the unfulfilled needs they carried with them from their parental families that led to expectations that the spouses could not meet."[9] Their vulnerability narrowed their capacity, singly and as a couple, to deal with change and to cope with stress. My own clinical experience very much bears out the findings of the Lidz studies. Examples of change and stress include pregnancy, the birth of a child, a career change, a significant loss, and the reduced possibility of interacting with one another because of work and travel demands.

We should all note, whether or not we are in the situation, that being a single parent makes a difference! All those emotional, physical, and intellectual challenges of parenting fall on one individual. That person does not have readily at hand another adult with whom she or he can compare notes and strategies. Nor does that person have someone with whom he or she can ventilate feelings and frustrations. A single parent has far fewer available resources when ill, depressed, lonely, or simply exhausted. Even the many spontaneous moments of fun and joy with children usually must be experienced without adult sharing. Single parenting severely tests the tensile strength of the individual. Compared with parenting in couples, it is a brittle system. Objective evidence for this brittleness comes from a variety of directions, including the increased number of registered contacts single parents and their children have with the mental health system (inpatient and outpatient clinics in the public and private sectors).

There is another kind of single parent, perhaps more common even than the one who has no spouse or partner: the single parent whose spouse is so preoccupied or involved with things outside of the family that the active parent is left to carry on alone. This situation can in some ways be even more stressful than a true single-parent system because in the context of the other parent's lack of participation—be this for reasons of personality, illness, or work—dramatic hostility and resentments usually develop. (The only exceptions would be situations in which such a relationship was agreed on prior to marrying or having children.)

Enter the first child. Whatever the couple's life-style and style of relating to one another, if the child and the state of parenthood are desired by both husband and wife, this mutual desire removes one of the major obstacles to having a parenthood relatively free of anxiety, guilt, and depression. Indeed, this mutual desire fosters the potential for enjoying and growing in the role of parent. The possibility of the spouses working together in a coalition and developing through that coalition increased mutual respect becomes a reality rather than a dream. The dynamics of the family is set in motion. Child and parents interact in all the ways I have just described, with temperament, health, attitudes, and expectations all playing a part. The addition of each child, in terms of the energy and attention demands on the parents, proceeds in a geometric rather than an arithmetic progression: One child plus one child equals more than two children. This seems to continue until a certain level is reached variously reported by parents as five (or six) or more children. Apparently, at that point, many parents either have become so adept, or so numb, or have succeeded so well in training the older children to help care for the younger children that the family functions without additional stress except possibly from a financial point of view. How many children there are; how well the children relate to each other; the months or years between each child; and the presence or absence of emotional, physical, and intellectual problems—all dramatically affect the nature of the interactions within families, the flow of energy and effort, and the degree of freedom or restriction.

The family serves as a vessel within which a series of interlocking relationships and memories of relations are contained.

Within its compass are the children and the parents (and the parents' experiences themselves as children), as well as grandparents and other relatives with whom they frequently interact. More and more common in today's mobile society are those friends with whom one spends a great deal of intimate time and whose influence on the family is sometimes more intense than that of the blood relatives. Behaviors and thought processes and life-styles frequently are shared among such friends in today's society.

So, we must not forget that the family, which has such importance for parenting, is composed of significant components, "miniuniverses" of interaction. Each component is itself a complicated realm of issues, issues of such great interest that modern Western culture has produced small libraries of books and articles about each of them. Any formal attempt to study these family issues for the purpose of improving one's performance as a parent probably would interfere with that performance. Such scholarship should be undertaken only if it is primarily for the purpose of some special pursuit or intellectual interest such as the furtherance of a career. What parents must realize is that as individuals they are not, never have been, and never will be anything other than "compounded" of many things: the attitudes and expectations they brought to parenthood and their reactions, responses, thoughts, and impulses—all deriving from a rich combination of influencing people and experiences. All these factors must be considered when trying to understand behavior within families or when trying to modify for any reason the behavior of even one individual within a family.

THE IMMEDIATE COMMUNITY

If we give it a moment's thought, we will see that the community in which we live has a real, at times dramatic, influence on our behaviors in various life situations. Consider, for example, how the community modifies our parenting behaviors. An apartment-dwelling family and a family dwelling in a freestanding suburban home allow their children very different degrees and kinds of freedom. The former cannot responsibly open its apartment door to send the preschool or early school-age child out to play alone; the latter parents can responsibly send such children out to play by themselves, since they are sending them into a familiar back or front yard where they can be monitored quite well even while the parents are engaged in other activities. For the same two families, the levels of concern and the relevant issues may well be reversed once the children have become teenagers. The city family's teenagers may have many entertainment, educational, job, and peer-group activities available to them, and they can get to these on their own often via public transportation. The suburban family's teenagers have fewer options in all areas and must rely on their parents for transportation (or on the cars of their parents, with all the risks and concerns that this involves). Because of their fewer options, these suburban teenagers tend to cluster in idle groups in school parking lots, drive-in restaurants, and shopping centers. The example just given is but an inkling of the ways that communities influence family functioning and the parenting role. Profound effects on the ecology of family systems are wrought by things such as sanitation and health, population density, the availability of work, educational and cultural resources, the number and density of religious and community organizations, the crime rate, and the presence or relative absence of natural disasters (floods, hurricanes, tornados, earthquakes).

How rapidly a community changes in its occupants, traditions, and values has a continuing effect on friendship networks, the willingness of people to get to know one another, and to share. The reality and deep importance in our lives of this issue of stability must not be underestimated. With the continuing slowdown in population growth, the average American, in terms of age, gets older and older. Over the next ten years there will be an absolute increase in the number of children and youth, yet their representation in the total population will decrease. Such changes produce other changes (some predictable, some not predictable) in the nature and functioning of communities. Again, with respect to only one issue in parenting, the experiences of being a parent or child is very different in a neighborhood full of children and in one with few or no children. Metropolitan living has been the trend for some time and will continue to be so. It is evidenced by increases in community size and population density. Associated with this, however, is a movement of people, jobs, and money out of the inner cities to suburban population centers.

Communities change further as more and more women join the work force. This is affecting families, making the structure of the family (essentially a social structure within which the role of being a parent or guardian can be played) more precarious, more demanding for all.

At present, the majority (79 percent) of children and adolescents in this country continue to live with two parents in the same household.[10] This, the "traditional" family, tends to locate in a metropolitan area. Such traditional families are on the decline in the United States, partly because of the high incidence of separation and divorce—particularly among those under forty-five years of age. Consequent to this phenomenon we see an increase in "nontraditional" families. Indeed, by 1977, they accounted for 21 percent of all families with children under age eighteen. Such families fall into three general categories: those headed by biologic or adoptive mothers, those headed by biologic or adoptive fathers, and those headed by neither a biologic nor an adoptive parent. A factor in these changes is the number of women with jobs outside the home *in addition to* their household and child-care work. Almost half the women with children under eighteen years of age now find themselves in such a situation. Mothers with children younger than six years are notable in this trend, as are mothers who have executive roles outside the home.

Issues special to local communities (though they are issues for our national community too) blend with issues important to social and family functioning. I speak of problems that for many families are immediate and heartbreaking realities: active abuse of drugs and alcohol, runaway children and adolescents, child and adolescent abuse, teenage prostitution, the pregnancy of young teenagers, the increasing incidence of accidents, cultism, and suicide and suicide attempts. All these special issues are associated with social change and the community. They reflect and also produce community stress. They reflect and produce varying degrees of dysfunction in the family systems.

Facing these issues is an important first step in dealing with them. The data that follow suggest how widespread these problems are; they suggest, too, that parents should look not only to their children for an explanation but also to themselves and their communities.[11]

ALCOHOL ABUSE. Although alcohol abuse has traditionally been considered a problem of adults, it is well known that drinking usually begins in the teenage years. Only recently have alcoholism and alcohol abuse been recognized as increasingly present among young adolescents and even among those in their preteens. Seventy percent of the teenagers in the United States have tried alcoholic beverages. Of the approximately 16.9 million young people between the ages of fourteen and seventeen years, 3.3 million are estimated already to be problem drinkers. Occasional deaths secondary to acute poisonings do occur during drinking contests or as a result of "dares." In addition, there is a very close association between the use of alcohol and injuries and deaths in motor vehicle accidents. Indeed, recent studies in both the United States and Canada have shown that a lowering of the drinking age, combined with the ability to obtain a driver's license at as young an age as sixteen, has contributed significantly to an increase in automobile accidents and the morbidities derivative of these accidents.

PHYSICAL ABUSE. Following efforts by such physician leaders as Dr. Henry Kempe of the University of Colorado, the battered child syndrome has become a nationally acknowledged concern. All fifty states now have some laws on their books relating to child abuse and neglect. Less generally recognized is that physical abuse of adolescents is also an issue. Indeed, evidence has documented that about one fourth of all reported cases of child abuse actually involve youths between the ages of twelve and eighteen years. One particular study even reported that 58 percent of a sample of college freshmen had been physically attacked by their parents during the year prior to college; of these, 6 percent reported significant injury from such attacks. The relationship of abuse to later social acting out and frank antisocial behavior appears significant. One pair of researchers found that ninety-two out of the hundred first-time juvenile offenders studied had been abused in their families of origin; houses for runaways report similarly high levels of abuse among the teenagers who use them.

CRIME.   Juvenile crime is not confined to the lower socioeconomic classes, as cliché thinking would have us believe. Across the board there has been a frightening increase in the number of antisocial acts committed by people under the age of eighteen years. Even more disturbing is the rise in the number of those under age eighteen involved in the most serious acts. For example, during 1975, 43 percent of the total arrests made in this country were of those under age eighteen. The almost 1 million young people arrested who were under the age of eighteen represented 10 percent of all the individuals arrested in the country for murder, 11 percent of all aggravated assault, 9 percent of all forcible rape, 34 percent of all robbery, 53 percent of all burglary, 45 percent of all larceny and theft, and 55 percent of all motor vehicle theft. The relationship of social class to this socially deviant behavior does not fit into popularly held beliefs. For example, in one of the wealthiest counties in the United States, 80 percent of all robberies are performed by juveniles, many of whom come from extremely comfortable families.

CULTS AND CULTISM.   During the 1970s a flowering occurred of religious-type cults that specifically sought out youthful adherents. Youth-directedness is the norm for such groups, throughout at least Western history. We have no knowledge at a national level of the exact number of such cults nor of the number of youths involved in them. Every day, however, letters of pain and distress concerning the rejection of families or family values are received by members of Congress, the White House, and individuals in other parts of the executive branch of government. Distress is expressed about the cults' rejection of parental interest, their fund-raising techniques, their regimentation of members, their recruitment styles, and their philosophies and goals. The courts have become involved in civil rights and custody battles involving families and cult members or cult organizations. During 1976, at least one cult was publicly acknowledged to be the object of FBI, IRS, and Justice Department investigations. Although many stories abound concerning lives that cults have "ruined," there are a small number of stories about lives that have been "saved" by them. Clearly those cults that undermine an adolescent's ability to make decisions for him or herself damage that adolescent's growth and development; for a small number of adolescents cults or cultlike organizations provide needed structure without coercion and are thus helpful to them.

It is interesting that within our communities cults are accepted as part of the current scene: Witness the popular "cult" of personality associated with show people and musical groups. At another level, cults are part of history, as documented by studies of cults and sects during the Middle Ages in Europe, studies on the alienated German middle-class children (the "Wandervogel") of the early twentieth century, or even the institutionalization of fascism during the late 1920s and the 1930s. From the community's point of view, cults are accused of preying on the high anxiety states that young people experience in separating and individuating themselves from their families. (This accusation is, in many cases, an accurate one.) It is important to remember that cults have thrived during periods of dramatic socioeconomic change. The eleventh through the sixteenth centuries in Western Europe, for example, constituted such an era. Not too distant, in terms of our own lives, was the growth of Nazism in Germany; it took over an entire nation during a period of upheaval, rapid change, and troubled questioning by members of that society.

In general, cults thrive in times when popular needs are met by anything that seems to offer a sense of control, stability, and belonging. Such needs definitely contributed to the involvement of many individuals in the People's Temple of Reverend Jin. Jones. The more than 900 deaths—by murder and suicide—that occurred in Jonestown, Guyana, during one day in November 1978 brought to international and national consciousness the issue of cults. An extraordinary event, even in the context of world history, the Jonestown deaths underlined the negative dimensions of cults, of certain human group behaviors, of planned recruitment, and of the retention of those recruited through such techniques as brainwashing, coercive persuasion, and mind control (all synonymous).

These issues have been with us for centuries, but in our time new developments have raised ominous questions about the possibilities for manipulating group and individual behavior, particularly with respect to personal autonomy and integrity. These developments derive from modern science—through electronics, chemistry, and the insights of behavioral sciences. All these are powerful tools which allow the influencing, indeed the controlling, of human behavior. Perhaps, thanks to Jonestown, these many important issues will now receive needed, ongoing public consideration and scrutiny.

RUNAWAYS.   Estimates over the past three years indicate that approximately 1.5 to 2 million children and adolescents leave their homes as runaways each year. Some of these youths, indeed, do not run away but have been "invited" in various ways to depart from the family scene. In general, they tend to come from home situations where they are frequently blamed for parental problems, where the father was absent or deceased, where the wage-earning parent (mother or father) was unemployed, where the family lived in a mobile home, or where alcohol or drug abuse existed among the parents. Mostly female but even occasional male runaways become part of a population preyed on by the pornography and prostitution industries. Resources for runaways include not only the development of special juvenile units within local police departments but also hot lines, teenage drop-in centers and health clinics, group foster homes, and runaway houses. Today it is the mark of a sophisticated community with good resources and sound reality testing when a combination of such facilities is available. Such facilities definitely reduce the number of possible tragedies and increase the possibility of children returning to the families they have left.

What can you as parents do about alcohol abuse, crime, child abuse, cults and cultism, and runaways? True, none of these issues may directly involve any of your children. However, neither you nor your children can avoid them, whether the children attend the most exclusive and reclusive private school or a good public school. As you will hear me say many times but in different ways throughout this book, the first important thing to do is to not pretend that simply because you are not aware of your child being involved in any of the above problems, such problems therefore do not exist for you. They do! As a responsible parent in today's society you must recognize their existence, learn about them with your spouse, ask your children what they hear and learn about them (from friends, teachers, reading, other places), and talk about them occasionally when appropriate—no sermons or lectures, please—in the family. They also should be topics for information gathering and discussion among friends and neighbors, as well as in the community (PTA or a private-school parents' association, community meetings, camps). Know what is going on around you and in your children's schools, after-school activities, camps, and colleges. Such knowing and involvement serve as great protections against unhappy surprises.

THE NATIONAL COMMUNITY

As you may have gathered, I strongly feel that the major issue for our national community is that of rapid social change. Many eras have witnessed dramatic social change, but ours is uniquely the "age of electronics." Products ranging from television and telephones to photo-offset printing and telephone-copying machines have produced an enormous flow of information among communities throughout this country and throughout the world, and they have also dramatically altered the roles of parents and teachers and their spheres of influence over children and each other. These are subjects about which books have been written and about which more will be said in the form of magazine articles, television documentaries, and special newspaper reports. For the purposes of this book, I believe it is important to pay short but particular attention to two dimensions of our national community: the media and the newer issue of children's rights.

The Media and the Family

Humanity knew very little when I was young. People did not know much about the rest of the world. From time to time there were travellers' accounts about people in other places, but by and large everybody saw and thought only about their local townsfolk or farm neighbors. The world was local. . . . Television amplified humanity's information-acquiring and -correlating capability over a million-fold.[12]

These excerpted 1974 statements by the architect and popular philosopher Buckminster Fuller capture quite well the changes brought to human lives by that superdevelopment called television. Reflections on the education and socialization of children in the Western world are frequent in our culture. One thinks of the French philosopher-writer Rousseau, of Wordsworth's "The Child is Father to the Man," of Schopenhauer's "There is no absurdity so palpable that it may not be firmly planted in the human head if you only begin to inculcate it before the age of five," and of Walt Whitman's "There was a child went forth every day, and the first object he looked upon, that object he became."

One of the major teachers of children in the United States is television. Over 95 percent of the households in the United States have at least one operating television set. Although the amount of time children watch television ranges from a few hours per week to eight hours or more per day, the average time the American child spends watching TV, according to various surveys, is approximately twenty-four hours per week. Preschool children watch television about four hours per day, and adolescents about two hours per day. Obviously, the degree of influence television has on children depends not only on the program content but also on the amount of time spent, the developmental stage of the child, and the nature and quality (pleasurable or not pleasurable) of the exposure.

Television does provide heightened visual and informational input. It allows its viewers to experience people, places, action, and social behavior that they would not otherwise experience. It allows the presentation of products through advertising in such a manner that their appeal is heightened beyond what it might ordinarily be, an appeal that the unsophisticated have relatively few defenses against. It is known that those under the age of seven years tend to retain less of the plots of what they see and more of the irrelevant details; they tend to learn fewer facts than do older children; they tend to accept as facts things that older children will not accept. Research studies concerning violence on television have shown irrefutably that it does result in increased aggressive behavior and use of aggressive solutions to interpersonal conflicts in children who are heavy television watchers. Socioeconomic status, race or ethnic group, or the sex of the child make no difference in this influence. Television is a powerful teacher that affects both the individuals and the family systems of all socioeconomic groups and almost all people in our country. It provides role models and lessons about causes and effects in the human and nonhuman world. It is also a powerful generator of expectations and an instructor concerning our material needs. As currently used, it tends to reinforce social stereotypes (such as sex roles) and social stigmas (such as our society's relative nonacceptance of people who are different, disfigured, or handicapped); it also instructs us, by the omission of the variety of possible human behaviors and interactions, in a certain inflexibility of spirit and intolerance of difference.

As a powerful teacher and socializing force, television obviously can and should be mobilized in prosocial ways. As a first step, parents must acknowledge the influence it has on the way they perform not only in their parent roles but also in their personal role and social roles. Further, parents should take an active interest in television programming and development, just as they have in the programming and development of the educational systems of our communities. This is of particular concern, since the norm currently appears to be one of parental noninvolvement. As reported recently, of "a sample of mothers of first graders in a California suburb, about 60 percent said that they never imposed restrictions on the amount of viewing. On the other hand, children's interpretations of TV commercial messages have been found to be highly susceptible to correctives provided by parents and other adults."[13] Community and national organizations have been developed to help families deal with the influence of television on children and families. The best known of these is Action for Children's Television (ACT). This group's work, combined with efforts by others, has had an effect on the television industry. For example, "the advertising time on Saturday mornings . . . has been reduced from 12 to 9 1/2 minutes per hour since 1973."[14] Yet the average child still sees about 21,000 commercial messages per year. Although there is evidence about the very positive dimensions that television adds to all our lives in terms of information exchange, entertainment, and even education, students of the issue do wonder to what degree it interferes, when not monitored, with the capacities of families and the individuals to use their time actively and to develop their own skills for discovery and independent learning.

The Issue of Children's Rights

Perhaps stimulated by the animal-protection movement, we have seen a great development in only the last twenty years in the child-protection (anti–child abuse and neglect) movement.[15] At least one student of the children's rights issue takes the following dramatic stand:

> Children are the last human beings who are treated as chattels. They belong to adults. Until 18 years of age in the United States . . . [they] indeed have no identity from a legal standpoint. . . . The child is powerless . . . forced to attend dull schools . . . forced to observe the hair-length commanded by adults who own him. . . . The food he eats is regulated by adults. His hours of retiring and awakening are forced upon him by adults. His bathing, his bodily hygiene, as well as his religion and politics, are all dictated to him by parents. What he does with his genitals, his sexual behavior, is controlled and tabooed by the adults who own him and his body. Furthermore, *nobody* can be physically beaten with impunity in our social system, *except children.* . . . Our record of oppression of children is a ghastly one.[16]

Whether or not one agrees with this statement of an intense professional child advocate, the issue of children's rights has, particularly since the late 1960s, grown dramatically. In 1967 a judicial decision (*In re Gault*) determined that children do warrant counsel and due process in a fashion similar to adults. Since that time, legal actions on behalf of children have snowballed. We find children suing their parents for poor parenting and requesting court-appointed foster parents, adult children suing parents for improper care while they were juveniles, and parents being brought before magistrates on the basis of the reports of neighbors or school systems that they have abused or neglected their children.

The Supreme Court has become and will continue to be involved in these issues through cases such as *Kremins* v. *Bartley*, in which the constitutionality of statutory provisions in a particular jurisdiction of Pennsylvania were challenged because those provisions permitted the commitment of juveniles to institutions for the mentally retarded simply on application of parents or guardians, regardless of the wishes of the juvenile and without requiring a hearing or other due process protections. In another case before the Supreme Court at the time of writing this book (*Parham* v. *J. L.* and *J. R.*), the issue, this time for the state of Georgia, is being reviewed as to whether state health procedures are unconstitutional violations of juvenile patients' rights. Should children in such situations have access to independent counsel and representatives? What rights do parents have to make decisions "on behalf of their children"? What are the traditional rights and powers of the family? Earlier it had been decided by various court decisions that the state may intervene with regard to parental decisions where those "decisions will jeopardize the health or safety of the child, or have a potential for significant social burdens."

The state is recognized as having interests superior to those of parents when it seeks to protect battered or neglected children or when it requires regular school attendance or vaccination or emergency medical treatment. To many of us, at first glance, children's rights seem to relate only to special situations or "other people" in the population. This is a misperception. Children's rights will continue to evolve as a movement. Parents who are executives will be involved as much as others as a continuing reexamination and even a redefinition of parental roles and authorities occurs. This will affect not only those of us who have children with special situations (mental illness, severe mental retardation, emergency medical care needs, pregnancy) but also all of us in terms of our relationship with our children and the interactions within our respective family systems.

4

Behaviors Essential to Caring

We are in a time in the United States when historical and cultural forces have conspired to make the raising of children a very self-conscious process. Parents search for "right ways" to proceed in matters of nurturance, education, discipline, community participation, and family interaction. They engage in self-conscious scrutiny of their performance on all these counts, and consequently lose touch with their nurturing feelings and instincts. Indeed, parental responsibilities seem almost overwhelming when listed in this fashion! What, then, becomes of the fascination, the richness, and the joy of being a parent?

Finding an "antidote" to this sense of unease about parenting may seem a major undertaking. Certainly the cultural and social forces working against it are powerful. We discussed in the previous chapter a first step in freeing oneself from these forces, that of recalling and daydreaming about one's own child-

63

hood—a critical and not so easy process: "All grown-ups were once children although few of them remember it."[1] In this chapter we will consider some further ways to gain or regain comfort in the role of parent.

Parents are instructed all the time about good parenting behavior and bad parenting behavior. These instructions—by knowledgeable and sometimes not-so-knowledgeable authority figures—have helped to generate fads. Faddism almost approaches the status of a chronic disease in the United States, affecting everything from child rearing to diet and exercise. Various child-rearing rights and wrongs have been enthusiastically embraced; a tendency toward overenthusiastic application of early scientific reports that began in the 1920s is still going strong.[2] Most recently we have been instructed about "critical periods" and postbirth child development. An example is the newly popular doctrine that mother-infant contact (preferably skin-to-skin) during the minutes and hours immediately after birth makes a *critical* difference in the development of the parent-child relationship and hence in the child's development.[3] Yet our history reveals that human beings, young or old, are more elastic than theories of critical periods or behaviors imply. We have greater capacities for adaptation and correction, greater tensile strength than those theories that expound all or nothing at a specific time would allow as the true ontogeny of human behavior.

Certainly, timing is important (as it is in all human endeavors). Certainly, some actions (in kind and quality) produce better results than others. But there does not exist a biologic or human system which lacks the potential for modification and self-correction. Thus, parents must find their roles both simple and complex. They certainly should attend as they wish to the different explanations and recommendations of experts and scientists. While doing so, they must realize that studies are based on particular populations—often representing particular subcultures—and are conducted over limited time and that studies, by necessity, usually are held in controlled laboratory or clinical conditions. Most of all, parents should make their own observations of their children, attending to them, thinking about them, and talking to and about them. As one wise child development researcher recently stated: "Much of what a parent needs to know can be learned from observing and listening to the child."[4] Having thus put you on your guard, this particular expert now ventures some comments on several of the necessary behaviors by parents. Among parental concerns, these are the ones that have "top priority," as my executive readers might say. Remember, they relate primarily to the processes of caring, not to the production of a predetermined product (although all parents have such fantasies). (George Will, the columnist, put such fantasies in perspective when he wrote: "You see why I'm bitter about parenting? You try to nurture Mozart, and you wind up with Groucho Marx."[5])

NURTURANCE AND PROTECTION

What should parents do to protect and nurture their offspring? Most parents work out the answers to that question through the very adventure of being a parent. Fortunately, they can bring to the job their own keen memories of childhood: their hurts, fears, and joys. Their wish to give their children as much ot the good and as little of the bad forms the basis of their protective behavior as parents. In addition, they learn much by comparing observations and experiences with other parents. They gain perspective on the things that cause them worry or apprehension; they learn different approaches to specific problems. Indeed, this kind of sharing with other parents may be often as good as a direct line to the best wisdom of the experts in child development. In contrast to this kind of sharing are "old wives' tales," meaning those "shoulds and musts" about proper parental behavior, as well as those explanations about child behavior that are so removed from current observations that no one recalls their origin, their validity deriving from repetition.

Perhaps the hardest part of protection is this paradox: In order to learn and to develop coping and other survival skills, children must be allowed, must even be encouraged to explore. Making mistakes, even having accidents, must be allowed. Yet we do not want children to make major or irreversible mistakes; we do not want them to have serious accidents. Where, then, does responsible protection begin and end? What kind of protection inhibits a child at different ages? How do you know if you are protecting a child from a probable, objective reality or if, in truth, you are projecting onto the child your own anxieties, insecurities, and fears?

Certainly, in practicing responsible protection we take into account the developmental stage of the child, whether infant, toddler, preschooler, grade-school-age, or adolescent. We consider also the situation of the moment—how familiar it is, how predictable the associated events. We follow culturally accepted norms in deciding when children can learn to swim, start school, be left alone at home, get driver's licenses, etc. Indeed, our culture largely defines "responsible protection" for us in the ideas it holds about what things children are to be protected from, how responsible they may be considered at certain ages, and so forth. Some guidelines can be offered for responsible protection, so long as we remember that multiple variations are possible.

Responsible protection concerns itself primarily with physical and emotional issues. It also relates to a certain training in values and ethics that provides reference points and explanations of reality. From the physical point of view, obvious issues include those of nutrition (no longer a simple issue), clothing, and recognition that a child is hurt or ill and provision of necessary care. Responsible protection includes education about rain, heat, snow, cold, the sun, and the effects the elements can have on us. (Recall those teenagers in Pennsylvania some years ago who permanently blinded themselves while "tripping on acid" during the last eclipse of the sun; they were lying on their backs staring up at the sky.) Education involves what all of us do when we talk to our children about animals, explaining that some dogs are friendly, and others not so friendly (this is no laughing matter; historically, many serious injuries occurred to children who teased dogs in eighteenth- and nineteenth-century America and England), or that they shouldn't try to pet the friendly wild squirrel, etc. Education also involves discussions with school-age children about "not accepting candy" or rides or other offers from strangers and what one should do if such people are encountered. With adolescents, responsible protection includes educating them about hitchhiking, its risks, and how such risks can be increased by the kinds of clothes that are worn. It means giving them information on sex, drugs, alcohol, driving, and consumerism.

Protection that inhibits a child means protection that is unrealistic for some reason. It implies a lack of acceptance of a child's competency to assume the particular risks of the situation. If we have been teaching them all along how to take care of themselves, we should be patient to see how they use what they have learned. Children do reach a point where they know what clothes to wear on a cold day, how to cross a street, where it is safe to walk at night, and the dangers of rock climbing or hitchhiking. They know these things and know that if they need more information they can ask for it. If children are ready, parents with courage and good judgment will let them "fly," realizing that to hold them back may work for a while but will eventually create tension and hostility. Such parents know, too, that they cannot protect their children against unfortunate, unpredictable occurrences.

This leads us to the question of how we can tell if some situations present truly harmful potentials to our children or if we are seeing things that way because of our own projected anxieties, insecurities, and fearful memories. All parents have some of these anxieties and fears. Our greatest help in finding the right balance in all this comes from the children themselves. As we know, children frequently protest our limit setting and intrusive concern, but they don't know what we know by virtue of our experience and perspective. If we allow children's protests to determine our behavior, we abrogate our responsibilities as parents, with all that that implies. It weakens the framework of trust within which children are able to develop, and, consequently, it can weaken the children themselves.

However, while we should not be ruled by their protests—their "nos," their "I won't do its," and their "do I have tos"—we should not be deaf to them either. Most such expressions are age-appropriate, predictable resistances to parental authority, ways of testing limits, and attempts at gaining control. If we pay them due attention, they can tell us much about the child's level of maturity. The age of the child and the context in which resistance is expressed and how it is expressed in words and behaviors (including the "nonverbals" of facial expressions)—all can serve as important signals to us that we may be imposing limits that are not objectively appropriate. If you are unsure, don't dismiss that uncertainty. Ask your spouse for his or her opinion. If your uncertainty continues or if there is important disagreement with your spouse, the viewpoint of others may give you the needed perspective. Those others may be family members, close friends, teachers, and pastors, as well as the children's friends and the parents of their friends. (I am not being specific here, since the situations in question will vary both from family to family and with the age and developmental stage of the child or adolescent. Thus, situations can include how close to keep a toddler at your side while shopping, whether or not to allow unsupervised play on "jungle gyms," imposing curfews, supervising slumber parties, giving driving permission, and screening employers of teenage children.) Only in the most dramatic situations will it be necessary to seek professional counseling.

There will be times when, after some thought, you feel certain that the protectiveness you are exercising is reasonable and responsible, even though most other parents in the community are not placing the same limitations. Such situations may simply reflect the fact that you have different values concerning behavior or different values concerning parental involvement and responsibility. If after examining your values they seem right and feel right to you, stick by them!

Each individual parent must develop reasonable judgment concerning issues of protection. It takes judgment to know when to trust one's children and courage to give them even reasonable degrees of freedom. In my practice, when problems arise for parents about overprotecting their child or adolescent, the major causes come either from unworked-out fears based on their own childhood experiences and misadventures or on fears they learned from *their* parents. Or they have lost, for any number of reasons—which can include high anxiety derivative of crises in their own lives—the capacity to trust in positive outcomes.

Obviously it is with adolescents that parents experience the most frequent failures in courage. The opportunities that children have to be influenced by others, the possibilities for travel by various means far away from home, and the possibility of exposure to substances of abuse and to sexual abuse are all major issues in our society today. They did not exist in the same degree and for so many people in this country before this age of instant communications, jet travel, and the automobile.

Courage thus involves the kinds of issues that belief systems organize for each of us, questions of life and its unpredictability and one's control over it (questions about which the world's religions offer various culturally shared understandings). Belief systems help us to live with uncertainty and with unpredictable contingencies or luck. They help us live with the reality that "Events do not occur as parts of a premeditated plot. To be sure, they always have their causes; they throw their shadows before them. But some . . . come to unsuspecting people with explosive suddenness."[6] Herein lies the need for courage and for some way to deal with the existential reality that our control of events and of people (including our own children) has very real limits.

DISCIPLINE

Closely related to protection are the issues of discipline and limit setting, which also involve early education and teaching. Again, we are dealing with questions that are simultaneously complex and obvious, clearly overlapping and subtle. Many families today are uneasy with questions of discipline and limit setting. Their discomfort shows in all manner of ways: letters to guidance columns such as Ann Landers or Dear Abby; complaints that schools do not provide enough discipline; anger and frustration over the influence of television; and confusion over how to deal with objectionable behaviors in or outside the home. Our society apparently is experiencing a "crisis of discipline."[7] And this crisis cannot be called the "fault" of parents. It has somehow evolved through the participation of everyone: expert educators, child development researchers, psychiatrists, and psychologists. This evolution was amusingly captured in the following pithy fashion by a poster in a Washington, D.C., toy shop. The poster, entitled "Advice to Parents,"[8] reads as follows:

1910———Spank Them
1920———Deprive Them
1930———Ignore Them
1940———Reason with Them
1950———Love Them
1960———Spank Them Lovingly
1970———THE HELL WITH THEM!

In my own practice I experience various forms of this "crisis of discipline." For example, in working with certain adolescents referred to me for their changes in behavior at home and school, I find these young people involved in sexual acting out, drug "tasting," and general surliness. My approach to them involves insistence on the adolescent suspending such behaviors *as part of the contract for working together* in exchange for my listening to him or her and dealing directly and in confidence with what is shared. Those who accept this contract show great relief and a reduced frequency of the undesired behaviors. To the parents and others there appears to have been some "magic" worked in therapy. The reality is that those adolescents were selected for their capacity to respond to clear, unambivalent limit setting from a firm but warm adult figure. Two things occurred: First, something was given (a special kind of attending) in exchange for that act of self-control on the part of the adolescent; second, an unconscious, or conscious but not articulated, desire for having limits set was recognized by the therapist and was made a major element of the initial therapeutic strategy.

The desire, indeed the need, for having limits set exists in all of us! It helps to remember this and to incorporate it into your interactions with your adolescent. Realize that most adolescents, even when their behaviors are extremely upsetting to us, are quite normal. Their behaviors are not random events. An adolescent's emotions are intense, and often the feeling states that she or he has are composite, even containing polar opposites such as shame and triumph.

Adolescents need warm, interested, adult parents. But "warm and interested" combined with "all-accepting" is at the least unhelpful to them and sometimes harmful. Being firm, clear in articulation of your expectations, willing to explain (but not debate) your values, and sincerely willing to listen helps enormously in families and may spare you the need for intervention by therapists. This is true despite the much greater complexity of the family system compared to the therapeutic relationship. Also, it is in the context of the adolescent and the parent being clear with each other about boundaries that positive interactions can occur. (Here, the greatest responsibility rests on the parents' shoulders, since by definition adolescence is a time when boundaries should be shifting, even frequently.)

The situation obviously becomes different when any of the parties involved are truly emotionally ill—that is, that they have some chronic affective disorder such as depression or a chronic disorder in thinking which interferes with their testing of internal and external realities. In such situations skilled professional help is usually required.

Discipline and limit setting organize reality. Experience with them should be tailored to the developmental level of the child and should begin with early childhood. When exercised consistently and clearly, with appropriate methods that avoid physical harm or inappropriate intrusiveness and control, both discipline and limit setting result in reduced anxiety and a greater sense of self in the child. Quality behavioral science research studies on children as they developed confirm this "truth"—a principle that wise grandparents already knew. Ongoing studies begun in the mid-1960s by child development researchers at the University of California indicate that firm, consistent, rational, and issue-oriented limit setting was associated with "responsible, assertive and self-reliant behaviors in preschool children."[9] Other forms of parental behavior do not produce so clearly such characteristics in children.

The setting of limits and the use of discipline are true skills. Parents must know clearly what the limit setting or discipline is for and the reasonableness of it (to themselves, the child, and others). The same limits and the same style and consistency of discipline should be practiced by both parents. As with lower animals, discipline whimsically imposed does not work. Instead, it tends to increase the potential for abuse as a result of the parents' frustrated rage at its lack of success.

Parental style in discipline has to do with the methods used; these fall basically into the categories of verbal discipline, physical discipline, deprivation of privileges, and isolation from others. Parents should use the measures or combination of measures that they find most comfortable and effective. They should never forget that any of these measures has the potential for being abusive and damaging. For example, spanking as a form of physical discipline can be acceptable and effective without being in any way abusive; it can also kill. Isolation from others, as another example of disciplining, can be effective without harm; it can also be punitive and psychologically damaging.

Parents need to be clear about their roles: They are primarily parents, not the pal or friend of their child or adolescent. Parents need to purge themselves of certain common misunderstandings, which range from thinking of discipline and limit setting as necessary evils to equating discipline with fear. Children are not programmed in their genes to know what is dangerous to touch, eat, and move toward or over. Likewise, they do not know the mores and acceptable behaviors of any society. These must be taught, and teaching involves saying no, showing that if you do this, others will reject such behavior and that therefore you must not do it. Touching, tasting, and going toward dangerous things are natural for a young child. Taking attractive things, things one wants, is natural. Lying (for what is lying in the young other than pretending that something is different from the way it is) also is natural. We all start life without control over our own physical reactions and aggression. It takes years before we have a sense that injury or death cannot be conjured up or made to disappear on a wish. Each child has a different natural capacity for attending, listening, and focusing attention. To gain skills, all these capacities must be modified. In short, discipline and limit setting are not only critical to socialization and education, but they determine the nature of any society.

As the child proceeds in his or her life, limit setting must continue but in modified form. The roles of male and female figures are important in this process. Ideally, the quality and specifics of limit setting should change in parallel with the developmental stage of the child or adolescent. They should be tuned to the child's or adolescent's rhythms, temperament, and coping style. With the adolescent, authority based on rational (understandable to the adolescent) concern is acceptable in our culture. Authority, discipline, and limit setting are not acceptable if the adolescent does not intellectually grasp the reason and the concern or if the parents' underlying motive is based on a drive for dominance and power (that is, "I'm stronger, smarter, more experienced, have more economic resources than you have"). Discipline does not work with adolescents if they have not had experience with it earlier in their lives.

In addition, let us remember that our society is one of seductive, apparently unlimited expectations, of rapidly changing family structure, and of "small" wars and the constant vague threat of nuclear holocaust. The resultant anxiety produces in many people an increased need to feel part of something and through that belonging to be structured. This need is most intense for those who are in the midst of the dramatic developmental transitions of adolescence. When not met, this need translates into the "crisis of discipline" seen within many parts of our social structure and within families—deprivation of institutionalized and internalized controls over anxiety and the stresses of uncertainty.

Parental authority, like the authority of executives, derives from both real and apparent powers. As parents, we have power based on our physical size, strength, knowledge, skill, and familiarity with the social system's structure, taboos, and values. In considering our behaviors we must not forget this power, particularly that our children in experiencing it integrate it as part of their memories and psychological structures. These powers remain permanently, actively integrated as direct memories and symbolic representations long after at least the physical basis of our powers has faded. Finally, we must all remember that power derived from simple physical strength or control of material things has a short life in most modern families.

TEACHING/PLAYING

Necessary parental behaviors include spending time with children during which we make eye contact with them, we listen with attention, we respond in a way that reflects that attention, and we appropriately touch. These nonverbal and verbal behaviors strongly communicate caring, warmth, and love. No monologues on our interest and love, no matter how eloquent, and no gifts or excursions, no matter how expensive or elaborate, have the strength of these behaviors; indeed, their power is so great when they are sincerely part of our interaction with a child or adolescent (indeed with anyone of any age) that they make the time spent with that individual infinitely more memorable and important.

In all children, learning occurs unless considerable efforts are made to prevent it. Children, like all young mammals, are curious from birth: They scan with sight and hearing and smell and touch their environment, seeking out the sources of all stimuli and fixing attention on them. Children have not only a capacity but also a drive to learn. This capacity is an interactive one. Children naturally delight in sharing their curiosity and in questioning. To parents, the challenge becomes one of understanding, guiding, and enhancing this drive. Understanding the process of learning becomes critical for parents because in families it takes two forms: that which is conscious and deliberate and that which occurs without such control and awareness though having greater effects. Parental style affects both forms of learning. In teaching about things and experiences, the aggressive, intrusive, all-controlling adult generates tension, anger, and negativism in his or her child. Desires for learning and relating to others through learning are dampened by such an approach. On the other hand, a parent who is basically relaxed can comfortably share with his or her child. Such parents find themselves able to observe and listen to their children; indeed, there is often much pleasure in this process. Through such observing, combined with listening and appropriate responding, we encourage expression and exploration and teach mastery of the environment. Occurring beyond the awareness of most parents and children are those dimensions of learning that begin very early and involve everything from an internalized sense of being able to control events to a sense of gender identity (sense of maleness or femaleness). Within the family, beyond the awareness of most parents and of their children, powerful messages are conveyed concerning reactions to experiences, the expression of emotions, and reactions to emotions. It is through experiencing their parents over time that children and adolescents develop their styles of coping with the various challenges life presents to all of us.

5
Situations of Special Stress

Few of us live out our lives without experiencing some situation of uncommon stress—some unpredicted or unfamiliar event that strongly challenges our coping capacity. To survive the challenge, we find it necessary to mobilize all our resources, not only on our own behalf but also for our spouse and children. (They need extra efforts and sensitivity at times of particular stress.) The nature of the events I speak of can vary widely, but in general they fall into two categories: those that make dramatic immediate demands and those whose challenge varies in its drama but continues for long periods of time. Among the former events that "serve up" a more time-limited challenge are separation and divorce, moving, natural disasters, death, and other losses. Among situations presenting a more continuing challenge are physical abnormalities from birth or from trauma that leave permanent damage of some kind, intellectual slowness (mental retardation, the exceptional child), severe learning or reading disorders, and serious emotional or psychiatric problems.

All uncommon stresses tend to identify the sufferer in some way. The individual identifies him or herself in terms of that suffering and is so identified by the community. Such distinguishment always has certain negative dimensions—some degree of stigmatization. Hostile or negative feelings (including fear) are strongly associated with stigma. As a result, stigma itself produces further stress, so that coping becomes even more difficult. Stigma is felt within the person and within those close to him; it is perceived as something projected from the community, and it is simultaneously expressed by the community through its behaviors toward the individual. Such are the internal and external dimensions of stigma, which hinder the seeking, accepting, and using of help by those undergoing these special stresses. Thus, we see how stigma is a major challenge to individual, family, and community health and why we all have a responsibility to work toward its elimination.

This chapter is concerned itself with several of those special life situations involving our children and our selves that dramatically drain emotions, sap energies, and test everyone's physical and spiritual strengths. Unlike situations of common stress, these situations either are not predictable or they have some unusually grave implications. These situations are the ones in which the need for help outside of oneself and outside of the family arises and must be recognized. Knowing when and when not to go beyond oneself for help is a major dilemma of our age.

CHRONIC MARITAL DISCORD, SEPARATION, AND DIVORCE

The most common expression of special stress *and simultaneously a major source of special stress* is chronic marital discord leading to separation and divorce. Executives and their families are no strangers to this phenomenon. We've reached the point in the United States where approximately one out of every five adults reading this book is divorced and has not remarried.

All of us are aware of the frequency of separation and divorce in the United States, but the statistics are surprising nonetheless. During the decade of 1960 through 1970, the divorce ratio (the number of divorced persons for every thousand people in an intact marriage) increased 34 percent. Between 1970 and 1977, the divorce ratio increased 79 percent! These increases are occurring at all social and economic levels.[1]

The majority of people who get divorces are under the age of forty-five years. Naturally, the number of children caught up in this phenomenon is significant.[2]

Remarriage is an active phenomenon associated with divorce: 83 percent of all divorced males and 50 percent of all divorced females remarry; 62 percent of these remarriages apparently last.[3] Besides having a lower incidence of remarriage, women as a group when they do remarry tend to wait a longer time before doing so.

Related in various important ways to separation and divorce are such issues as alcoholism and early (teenage) marriage. At least one study has associated prolonged unemployment, low fertility, and dramatic changes in one's health status (in either direction—improvement or worsening) with the dissolution of marriages.[4] Not infrequently the domestic disturbances of troubled marriages result in calls to police. As one indication of the intensity of feelings and their effects on behavior, consider this fact: On a national level 20 percent of police deaths in the line of duty are a function of fatal injury while responding to domestic disturbance calls.

Since we are talking about an issue that has serious implications for our future as well as for our present, I risk sharing a few more statistics: As many as a third of the children growing up in the United States during the 1970s are growing up in families that have been altered in some way by separation and divorce. Between 1970 and 1977, because of changes in our birth rate, the number of children under eighteen in this country decreased almost 5.5 million. During that same period, the number of children under eighteen who were living with only their mother increased 3 million. This is almost exclusively due to separation and divorce. By 1977, only 79 percent of all the children under eighteen in this country were living with two parents (not necessarily the original two). In separation and divorce, the children predominantly end up in the custody of their mothers. (This trend showed an increase of about 6 percent from 1970 to 1977.) Only about 1.5 percent of the children under eighteen who were living with only one parent lived with fathers in 1977.[5]

Why a Special Stress

The phenomenon of separation and divorce, although an increasingly common reality for our communities and ourselves, very much falls in the category of a special stress situation. The issues go far beyond ourselves to involve the intervention of at least the legal system and not infrequently the clergy or helping professions as well.

Divorces and separations, when combined with the high remarriage rate, are resulting in new forms of families and new styles of family interactions. Indeed, some students of "remarriage families" discern a form of pseudopolygamy in these situations of multiple divorce and remarriage where children are involved; for example, one male may have several wives (past and present) with whom he shares some form of parenting or support responsibilities and often social responsibilities derivative of these. Divorces and separations have heightened our awareness of custody as an issue in this society, an issue which involves the law, the child development community, the social services community, the child, and the parents. Basically, what we are talking about—if one sees the family as the smallest social and political unit in our society—are changes in that unit owing to shifts in relationships and authority lines that affect power balances. Such shifts can be handled with equanimity by some; they also can produce changes that make the system unrecognizable in comparison with its earlier form. For the individuals involved, the issues are complex. Let us look at just the main "players": the children and their parents, ourselves included.

For parents the issues are personal, social (including legal), and economic. The economics of separation and divorce can be very complicated, especially when child support is involved. Relatively recently, the federal government became actively involved in this problem by creating within the Department of

Health, Education, and Welfare the Office of Child Support Enforcement. (In 1977 that office collected $1.6 billion of previously unpaid-for child support by fathers of all social classes.) Related to issues of legal costs, child support, division of goods and establishment of new households, and even alimony are the changes and economic pressures felt by the men and women involved. Concerning women, today more than half of divorced women work full time.

Ours is an age of romantic marriage. People become and stay involved with each other because they are mutually attracted. Their legal liaison, or marriage, usually is based on that attraction and on a series of assumptions they make concerning each other, the nature of intimacy, and the way they will deal with evolving responsibilities. With luck and the absence of major stresses (such as chronic unemployment), most marriages still stay together. Those that do not usually end in separation and divorce—both lengthy and difficult processes.

The disintegration in the relationship may be visualized in terms of the iceberg metaphor. The nondevelopment of the marriage or the growing apart, can be far more serious than the surface indications would suggest. Even before the parties are consciously aware of it, their marriage may be in perilous condition. One early barometer of trouble is a definite, ongoing change in physical feelings toward each other and in sexual functions if such a change is not based on clear organic causes. There is no evidence that "affairs," "open marriages," and "swinging" prove salutory to troubled or apparently untroubled relationships. Indeed, even though there were claims in the 1960s and early 1970s that such activities resulted in more mature, stronger couples, those professionals who advocated such approaches and who continued to follow their effects have found that they actually undermine intimacy and trust. Because the disintegration of relationships proceeds so subtly, those who seek counseling for severe marital problems often do so when the relationship is *in extremis*. Indeed, often at least one member of the couple has basically made a decision to end the relationship and is really seeking divorce mediation rather than marriage counseling.

Ideally, couples who are having difficulties would be able to recognize such difficulties early, and would seek counseling. They would pay attention to the warning signs of a marriage in trouble. (These warning signs include repeated feelings of irritation toward your spouse when none existed before or in situations where you previously had no such feelings; more frequent arguments over any dimension or any combination of dimensions of daily life such as finances, repairs, child care; a continuing decrease in the amount of talking and sharing you do; and a change in the quality or frequency of your sexual relations with each other. Additional warning signs for executives include fights or angry withdrawals in response to any or all aspects of your work, including travel, business entertainment, and training.) In my experience, when warning signs are recognized for what they are, if the couple seeks help, at least 80 percent of those who originally found satisfaction in each other will be able, through counseling, to make the appropriate adjustments and growth steps needed to preserve the relationship.

Some relationships, however, are downright bad. Not infrequently such a marriage involves severe personality problems in one or both partners; the needs of one partner are met, at least partially, by the misbehaviors of the other partner. Extreme forms of this include the physical and psychological abuse of one's spouse. Wife abuse is now documented as a social problem for all economic groups in the United States. To quote from one source on this: "Police agencies in the East (San Francisco) Bay Region receive approximately 1,800 domestic disturbance calls monthly. Between 50 and 85 percent involve wife abuse. Knives, clubs, guns and other deadly weapons are found in slightly less than three-quarters of these situations. More than 100 battered women are admitted each month to seven East Bay hospitals surveyed by Rubicon."[6]

Of great poignancy, besides the stress and distress experienced by adults in such situations, is the issue of the effects on the children. Studies have been conducted which show a difference in the relations that divorcing parents and intact parents have with their children. These differences point toward a deterioration in the handling of children by divorcing parents. Such deterioration is understandable, given the issues that preoccupy mothers and fathers in these situations. However, sometimes the deterioration is dramatic, particularly in relationships where there is great animosity at work. In these situations children often are used as vehicles through which the parents communicate and fight with each other. Indeed, it is not unknown for a child to be used as a weapon by one parent against the other. Examples I have seen in my practice include children who were programmed by one parent to say damaging things about the other parent before judges and lawyers in exchange for special gifts, treats, or under threat of permanent rejection.

Before an actual divorce is executed, some kind of trial or formal separation is usually attempted. Only in rare instances does a divorce take place rapidly without prior process. Yet compared to what many individuals, their families, and friends engage in prior to marriage, the events of separation and divorce seem very private and relatively abrupt. When one thinks of the rather elaborate family and community supports that are involved with the process of getting married, one wonders what is being neglected when no such supports exist for individuals who are going through the even more stressful, no less public (in terms of people becoming aware of and reacting to the event) actions called separation and divorce. These actions might be more easily dealt with at the personal and family level if some form of ceremony or a series of rituals existed to help individuals and their relations and friends remove themselves psychologically and socially from a marriage. Such a clergy-officiated ceremony has been suggested recently in a book on divorce by Rabbi Earl Grollman and Marjorie Sams.[7] Some form of ritual or ceremony would not have to hinder the process of ending a marriage, but it could significantly help with stigma, unchanneled anger, and hostility; it could be tailored to the needs of the particular individuals and situations.

After the Fact

Following separation or divorce there are many challenges to parental and child adjustment. A major change in family relationships and power structure has occurred. The individuals involved have to struggle with such feelings as anger, guilt, resentment, ambivalence over the change in their status, and shame at having failed in something they once had high ambitions for; some may feel that they have been abandoned. For all there is some sense of failure and a concern, at least initially, as to whether they can function successfully on their own again. (This question of being able to function on one's own is often one of the things people test out in separations.) Individuals do not realize the extent of stress that divorce involves. For all there are transient physical and emotional symptoms. The mildest of these symptoms include tension and tension headaches, sleep disturbance, and excessive irascibility. For others, the physical and emotional problems may be more severe; they may suffer from colitis, skin problems, or depression with associated dramatic decreases in work and social functioning. Many men and women under age forty-five experience a short period of promiscuity in and around the divorce, evidently a kind of "necessary" period of acting out. For most this period passes rather quickly, and they end up labeling it as "boring" and "empty."

From the beginning, when children are involved, parents have to be concerned with economic provisions and custody arrangements and related issues, such as how one deals with holidays. In practice, these arrangements mean dealing with the children themselves and with oneself about their care. Bureau of the Census data reveal that the vast majority of the children from divorced parents are placed with their mothers. As a result, the fathers are made into "ex-parents" of a sort, whereas the mothers, who are suddenly plunged into the single-parent role, become overextended parents. The reality of this is so poignant that more and more couples seem to be moving on their own toward working out various forms of combined parenting even when official joint custody does not exist. I am joined by many professionals in encouraging such combined parenting whenever it is possible. It is better for all concerned. It helps parents to deal with issues of guilt, resentment, and anger within a more realistic context. It allows children a greater opportunity to understand and integrate the changes in the family relationships, the relationships between their parents, and their freedom from responsibility for the event. Current studies *do* show that the development of children is hindered by the absence of fathers. Thus, all reasonable efforts should be made to keep fathers involved, especially given the continuing reality that primary custody is usually granted to mothers.

If separation and divorce are a reality in your life, you must try to be sensitive to the age of your children as well as to their intellectual and temperamental resources. This means giving them explanations, and making particular efforts to emphasize that the problems primarily come from you and your spouse and that *they,* the children, are not responsible for *your* problems. Help them with their anger. Do not stimulate it by "using" your children as conduits of communication between your spouse and yourself. While helping them to understand that they are not the primary cause of the divorce, do not confuse them by being "on stage" with your "angst" in front of them. Particularly during the period surrounding and immediately after the divorce, if your children are in their midteens or younger, they need even more structure than they had in earlier years no matter what their ages. You can provide this by asking them to pitch in and help with the functioning of the now changed family; such pitching in can even be engaged in by preschool children. Parents must not, out of their own guilt concerning the situation, stop or let up on limit setting and discipline of their children. This would be interpreted as a sign of not caring or of not caring enough. Because of their own complex feelings and behaviors, it is not uncommon for parents to withdraw from their children, particularly in the period around divorce and shortly thereafter. We have the responsibility to be aware of ourselves, to observe whether or not we are engaging in such withdrawal. If we are, we must make efforts to stem that withdrawal; we should seek help with this if we cannot handle it on our own. It is possible to deal with divorce in a constructive way within the family, so that all concerned can end up feeling a certain pride in coping successfully with a difficult situation. This works, too, toward the benefit of long-term needs, such as the children's growth and development and the further growth and development of the parents, including their sexual, social, and career needs.

All children are affected by divorce. All children are aware, often before their parents, when things are gravely wrong in a marriage relationship. It is not unheard of for a child to spend years prior to the actual or official separation of his or her parents attempting to get the parents to relate to each other—carrying messages back and forth, weeping and pleading for them not to argue so much, and forming alternate alliances with one parent then the other. Because of their desire to see parents get back together, children are extremely vulnerable, particularly during the early phases of a divorce, to manipulation by their parents; in most situations, any taking of sides by children during such periods should be seriously questioned as to its genuineness. Evidence exists that family discord or disharmony in these situations produces a kind of stress and disruption in the development of children that is greater than that produced in other, more dramatic (to the society) circumstances such as death. One study shows that chronic discord and disharmony leading to divorce and separation is a significant loading factor in the delinquency of children.[8]

Again, all children in such situations are affected. They suffer from grief, anger, anxiety, guilt, and shame. They are resentful; their school performance often decreases; they often have psychosomatic problems, particularly those involving the stomach or intestine such as vomiting and diarrhea; and they often engage in various forms of attention-seeking behavior and this may indeed include aggressive antisocial behavior. These children, whether they be school-aged or adolescent, suffer from depression and loss of self-esteem. They often are afraid to express (particularly the very young child) their feelings. This lack of expression relates to their loss of control in a critical area of their lives—their family. It also related to the fear they have developed as a result of losing one parent, a fear about loss of parent now made more poignant by the assumption that if they act out in a particular way the remaining parent may leave them. How adversely children are affected obviously depends on the degree of disruption and strife, the degree of constructiveness or nonconstructiveness of the divorce, the level of caring the former couple had about the parenting role, and the ages of the children.

Children often get solace from other children. This occurs quite commonly within sibling groups. However, they often can be cruelly teased by children outside the family. Indeed, the outside world, which includes other relatives, important friends, teachers, the schools themselves and peers, can have major salutary and stabilizing effects for children in such situations or they can be sources of further disharmony and disruption. What we know about the consequences of divorces has been alluded to in the preceding discussion. We do know that children and adults have temporary disturbances in their physical and psychological functioning because divorce is a major stress and such stresses are expressed in physical and emotional terms. Beyond this, not too much is objectively known. For most individuals the visible negative effects seem to disappear gradually over a period lasting approximately two and a half years. These negative effects appear roughly in the following sequence: (1) anger, irritability, disbelief, resentment; (2) general psychosomatic symptoms of anxiety (including problems with eating and sleeping), changes in school or work performance; (3) return of old problems, obsessions, "habit spasms" (tics and stuttering), decrease in self-confidence. We see these changes in children and adults. The sequence may vary a bit from person to person, and within the same person each problem may come and go. The earliest to arrive tend to be the earliest to fade. Since we all are creatures of memory, none of these negative effects is ever completely erased. It's just that for most people, over a period of two and a half years, anger fades, depression ceases to be a major mood, general health improves, and self-confidence and primary involvement with other things return.

Such effects last longer in male children, with female children and parents having approximately the same period of fade-out effects. One study on one population of children showed that 40 percent of them had significant disturbances as long as one year after a divorce.[9] We do know, however, that when parents pull themselves together and are functioning effectively in the new situation, the children mostly follow suit. We know also that parents who seem to have tremendous struggles with the change, who feel intensely guilty and angry about it, seem to be less sensitive to problems that might exist in their children and consequently are less available to help the children. No matter how the situations are handled, no matter what the age of the children when the divorce occurs, these children frequently will carry around for years in their heads and hearts fantasies about getting their parents back together again. It is important that the issues be worked out so that a measure of stability is achieved. Such matters as support payments, visitation rights, one's own work and social life, the child's school and social life, and adjustment to changed or new physical environment—how well all these things are handled will determine in important ways the well-being or impairment of the child in divorce.[10]

Helping the Child (and Yourself)

Parents in a divorce are often confused about what to do and when to look for professional help. Some generalizations can be made. As said earlier, ordinarily the children's relationships with both parents should be preserved.[11] This helps in their growth and development and makes them less likely to develop distorted "fantasy images of absent parents."[12] Such images, when they do develop, work against the child's resolving and understanding the situation; they may also contribute to psychological distortions in the child (including unresolved feelings such as anger or resentment) that will make it difficult for him or her to have healthy heterosexual relationships later on.

When there is some form of combined parenting, regular visitation should be worked out. This may present a special challenge to you the executive. Before a routine is established, you and your children need extra time. You will need more flexibility in your travel, evening, and weekend meeting schedules. The temptation will be to escape into work responsibilities at a time when the most appropriate behavior may well be to interrupt a morning or afternoon schedule to attend a school play or conference. Developing such flexibility in your schedule and life rhythms may require the aid and support of relatives, friends, colleagues, judges (when involved), and the teachers of your children. If no agreement can be reached about visitation and ways of shared parenting (cross-consulting about discipline, illness, injury, schoolwork, extracurricular activities, summer activities, etc.), then this situation is an appropriate one for professional intervention. The professional can help you reduce or eliminate communication problems and other conflicts that militate against the shared parenting. (It is not infrequent that such conflicts proceed from misunderstandings and inability to communicate existing within the context of good faith on the part of both parties.)

In helping children adjust to the situation, it may be most useful to call up the cliché of "action speaks louder than words." Explanations and statements of caring and interest are much less effective with children than are actions. The children will have confused feelings about love and hate. No matter what their age, they will have difficulty seeing that the departure of one parent is not the same as being unloved by that parent. They also frequently feel that somehow, in some way, they are responsible for the breakup of the marriage. Children need help in voicing these feelings and in adjusting to the reality of the situation. Sometimes the reality is that the parent leaves because indeed they are not loving or indeed they have a serious personality problem (it may be selfishness or a mental health problem such as alcoholism or drug abuse). In these situations, it is important that the children understand that something was and is wrong with that parent and that they may have to—as far as that parent is concerned—take Richard Gardner's advice and "look for love somewhere else."[13]

Children also need a great deal of help in expressing their fear and anger. They need help in realizing that it is all right to have these and other intense feelings, that it is all right to recognize such feelings. They also need assistance (as often do the parents) in learning that such feelings do not have to be dangerous, that there are ways of appropriately and nondestructively expressing them.

What parents do in limit setting and disciplining, such as getting their children involved in family chores, is good in that it provides organization and needed structure; but in a divorce situation parents will have a tendency to encourage their children to act more grown up than would be the case if the divorce situation did not exist. As a transient pressure this is acceptable; but as a continuing pressure, whereby children are encouraged to become too sophisticated, too grown up, too much in control, and too responsible too early, it is not helpful.

Related to limit setting and discipline is learning how to spend time with your children after your divorce—that is, spending time with them the way you might have (and hopefully did) prior to the divorce. You did not always try to do special or fun things or always give them treats. A lot of the time involved just being around each other while the children did their thing and you did yours, and it is important to return to this state. In doing so it is important, too, to help the children maintain their friends and friendship networks.

A traditional danger in the postdivorce period (traditional in the sense that it includes the stuff that fairy tales are made of) is the child's interaction with a stepfather or stepmother. All children of divorce receive such individuals with ambivalent feelings. Stepfathers and stepmothers are perfect setups for being made scapegoats, for being the sinks into which are poured all the angry and hostile feelings children might have towards their "real" parents. (Children see it as safer to express these feelings toward the stepparents than toward the parents to whom they are developmentally and emotionally bound.) Prior to marriage and remarriage and shortly afterwards much attention is needed on this matter. Sometimes transient outside counseling for all involved can prove helpful. The changed family interactions and relationships can work out well when the involved adults put great effort into listening to and learning the needs of the children and of each other. Such listening and learning obviously must be followed by appropriate behaviors.

The really unfortunate situations more often involve the divorced parents than the stepparents, especially when they have an ongoing hostility toward each other or a newfound hostility, as in reaction to the seeming ability of the former spouse to adjust to and even enjoy their new situation. Here, when there is combined parenting or some form of shared custody, children are in danger of being used as spies or tattletales in a tug-of-war, particularly over the issue of time sharing.

Divorce and divorce-remarriage cycles are so common now that they may be considered part of our popular folklore—an expected behavior, a kind of "norm." Certainly they have become a major force for change in family relationships within our society. I, for one, believe in neither passively accepting this phenomenon nor enhancing its development. When couples come to me for counseling, I work very hard with them in exploring how much of the relationship remains, how it can be developed and improved. Sometimes these explorations reveal that little is left for these individuals or that what remains is so tattered, stained, and shredded that to repair it would be too disfiguring to the individuals, the family, and the idea of "being a couple." Such couples have limited choices; the greatest wisdom for them and their children may be divorce.

Instead of cynicism about marriage and families, interest in the prevention of serious marital dysfunction is the best approach. This begins prior to marriage, in having as much understanding as possible about the married state. Equally important and intimately related is the clarification of your expectations. Clarifying and understanding your expectations, selecting potential partners based on them, and learning the potential partner's expectations—all are essential preventive preludes. Most people can engage in this attempt on their own. It takes only an awareness that it is important to do and the effort to carry it through.

Contrary to popular opinion, the upper socioeconomic classes have fewer divorces and a higher rate of successful remarriage when remarriages occur. This may relate to such factors as education, training in attending to and articulating expectations, or simply the good fortune of having fewer economic pressures.

When divorce does occur, remember that it involves intense challenges. All the resources that exist within you and your children should be mobilized. Successfully dealing with the major and long-lasting stresses can produce new strengths. As executives, realize that you have more resources of all kinds to draw on than most others have. You can use them to their fullest so long as you keep your priorities straight. Handing the "whole mess" over to lawyers and therapists and plunging into work does not represent keeping one's priorities in order; instead, this course will exact a very heavy price in pain, disappointment, and loneliness somewhere farther down the road.

DEVELOPMENTAL DISABILITIES

Autism, cerebral palsy, learning disabilities, and mental retardation are but a partial listing of developmental disabilities. They differ from one another in the kinds of dysfunctions present and in the causes of these dysfunctions. They are alike, however, in that they are diagnosed in childhood and that they render more difficult the development of the affected individuals.

As children with these disorders of function grow up, more and more problems arise for them as well as for their parents and families. This is a reality whether or not helpful professional interventions are received. Such interventions, when optimal, include working toward ameliorating the children's weaknesses or dysfunctions while at the same time enhancing their strengths.

These children must be approached from points of view other than simply their defined disabilities. They must be treated as participants in a family and community system. If dealt with in this fashion, while also receiving the best educational techniques we have to give them, the vast majority of such children can be significantly helped.

Mental Retardation

Approximately 75 percent of the mental retardation in this country is associated with socioeconomic deprivation (including everything from poor nutritional and health care to minimal learning opportunities).[14] Thus, mental retardation is not found with any great frequency among people of the upper socioeconomic classes. When it does occur among such people, most of the time it results from a genetic defect (such as mongolism, or Down's syndrome), a biochemical defect (such as Tay-Sachs disease), brain injury secondary to birth trauma, or an accidental trauma later in life. For the individual child and family affected, no matter what their socioeconomic status, "frequency" and statistics are absolutely irrelevant.

Having a mentally retarded child presents major challenges to the family. These challenges keep changing as the child ages. Since, for parents, their children represent extensions of their social and physical self-images, the mentally retarded child at first stimulates feelings in the parent of being imperfect. These feelings usually are rapidly followed by self-questioning such as "Why me? Why my child?" then by anger, bitterness, resentment, shame, and finally some form of acceptance of the reality.

Stigma looms as a very large issue. How deeply it affects a particular family will depend on several factors: how retarded the child is, whether there are other handicapping conditions, the age and emotional makeup of the parents, the existence of siblings and the state of their health, the attitudes and talents of the helping professionals and the community, and how early in the child's life mental retardation is diagnosed.

I have seen families cope quite well with children who have few capabilities beyond those of basic self-care. I have seen families frantic, depressed, angry, and in turmoil because they could not accept a child whose intelligence was limited but who was capable of much more than self-care. In many cases the needed adjustments involve the family's expectations of performance and self-image. (For example, not infrequently, a bright, competitive, achievement-oriented family has difficulty accepting a child of merely normal intelligence and average motivation.) This issue can be more of a barrier to improved functioning than any difficulties in securing "special education" or vocational training for a retarded youngster.

If you are faced with the problems of parenting a retarded child, remember that the term *retardation* covers many things. First, consult with the best professionals you can find. Obtain the best evaluations and explanations concerning what can and should be done. Use parent advocate resources such as the National Association for Retarded Citizens (Appendix B), as well as professional resources. In your consultations, seek not only information about the child in question but also about the implications for you, your spouse, your other children, your marriage, and the entire family system. Concentrate at first on gaining complete understanding of the problem and the immediate, needed interventions. Over time you will delineate the child's needs, the needs of his or her siblings, and your own needs. Much is known, and many resources are available for support and help.

PHYSICAL DISEASES AND ACCIDENTS

We experience most acute diseases as time-limited, rarely serious dysfunctions. When disease occurs that is both acute *and* serious, we are faced with the sudden, unpredicted onset of a potentially life-threatening illness. The course may last for days or a few weeks. Examples of such illnesses include pneumonia, meningitis, encephalitis, and diarrheal diseases of infancy. As you recognize, such disorders are now infrequent in the majority of our child population owing to the combined public health efforts of sanitation (food and water) and immunization. Outbreaks of acute, serious disease continue to occur, though the number of people affected is relatively small. When they do occur they are frightening to child, parents, and doctor. Admitting that fear and using it to mobilize oneself toward useful action are the best responses. Don't be reticent to "bother" the doctor or emergency room!

Prevention—through immunization, sanitation, proper nutrition, exercise, and rest—is the best way to deal with such disease. Second best is early recognition by parent, guardian, or teacher that "something is wrong." Prevention and early intervention combined should reduce to the vanishing point the modern community's experience with such diseases in their children.

Accidents exceed by far all other causes of permanent physical damage and death in the child population. Poisonings, motor vehicle accidents, drownings, and fire wreak the most havoc. Accidents are thus a major public health problem in the United States. For survivors of serious accidents, the sequelae include guilt, anger, and sometimes permanent body or brain damage. The emotional challenges to individual and family in such situations can be dramatic.

As trite as this sounds, accidents can best be dealt with by prevention. First, this means being truly, consciously aware that they can occur. Second, you should train yourself, your spouse, any other adult living or working in your home, and your children in accident prevention (see Appendix A). Finally, you should also train your family in first-step actions to take if there is an accident. The public service messages about fires, automobile accidents, poisonings, and falls should all be taken seriously.

CHRONIC ILLNESS AND DISEASE

Chronic disorders are those that last for a long time—perhaps for as long as the child lives. They include diabetes, kidney disease, certain forms of allergic disorders affecting the lungs or skin, cancer, heart disease, rheumatoid arthritis, and many other disorders. They require special adjustments—the development of special coping styles and modified goals— in all those involved. Expectations must be changed, flexibility must be enhanced as much as possible, and knowledge should be accumulated about the nature of the condition and how to deal with it. In such cases, involvement with the medical community expands to the point that it sometimes becomes a major element in family life. Children who have a chronic disease and their families often must struggle heroically to maintain their own integrity and sense of control.

If chronic disease is a reality in your life, do not give it completely over to the experts, be these expert physicians, special educators, or social workers. Educate yourselves and your children about the disease (no matter what it is) and its treatments. While emphasizing hope and function, participate as much as possible in treatments and rehabilitative efforts. This means everything from working to understand them as well as you can to expressing your opinion on the advisability of particular interventions. Beware of any health professional who wants to keep you or your child as dependent innocents. Chronic diseases respond best—meaning that people gain some ability to function in their lives—when they are dealt with from a shared, or team, perspective. Families must be part of that team, together with the patient and the medical personnel.

MENTAL HEALTH PROBLEMS

Mental health problems usually refer to behaviors by individuals that bother, disturb, frighten, and upset us. Lots of behaviors can fit such a description, sometimes fitting it because we are overtired, ignorant, or intolerant. By this I mean that aberrant behaviors and "crazy" behaviors do indeed have something to do with "the eyes of the beholder." Let's keep this caution in mind, recalling it as we observe not only those people outside of our family but also our own family members.

On a somewhat more subtle level, mental health problems refer to psychological problems that produce some ongoing interference with social functioning. In an individual this can mean depression or violent behavior or chronic shoplifting.

Within a family it can mean everything from a dramatic absence of interactions to very active, sadistic, and stormy ones. Mental health problems are considered a serious and relatively neglected issue in public health. An estimated 18 percent of all children from birth through age seventeen (12 million young people!) have such problems in the United States.[15] (The adult population with such difficulties would add another 22 million to this tally.)

Since most of our children are quite healthy, how do we know if they are developing an emotional problem? It certainly is not as simple as finding their behavior "disturbing"—you can't be a parent and not at various times be unhappy or upset or even "driven up the wall" by your child's behavior. But when is silliness a problem, hostility and disobedience a problem, destructiveness a problem, and shyness or sadness a problem? You yourself could add considerably to this list.

The interested, involved parent is the best "screening device" for such doubts. If you are uneasy about what you are observing or experiencing, check into the situation. Don't ignore your uneasiness! Observe your child more carefully, talk to other mothers and fathers with whom you have a good relationship, talk to the child's teachers, talk to the family physician or group health insurance physician, talk to a specialist (clinical child psychologist, child or adolescent psychiatrist). During certain periods in their development children have a greater probability of running into psychological and/or behavioral difficulty. Periods worthy of special attention include: infancy (does your baby relate and respond?); age four-five years; age eleven-thirteen; and age seventeen-nineteen. As very general guidelines, you should wonder if your child has or is developing some mental health problems if you observe any of the following: (1) He or she is not developing properly and there are no identifiable physical, physiological, or environmental causes for these problems in development. (2) Your child is not able to engage comfortably and successfully in the context of his or her intelligence, in the "work" of children—meaning school and play (relating to others). (3) Your child or adolescent changes dramatically for no objectively identifiable reason (including peer pressure) in how he or she relates to the family, school, and peers, *and* this change lasts for more than a few weeks.

The majority of mental health problems occur in response to stressful situations. Hence, no matter how dramatic they are in their overt expression, they eventually resolve, though often leaving their mark in some form of future vulnerability. All can be treated and improved if dealt with early and appropriately. Successful treatment for children and adolescents involves the parent and the family system in some way. Interactions among family members have proven critical, even when one is dealing with conditions like the schizophrenias, where the principal dysfunction seems to clearly reside in one person. When worked with properly, the family can be a refuge, a place for healing and strengthening.

Particularly to the busy, work-involved parent I repeat: Do not look for emotional problems at every sign of irritability, irascibility, rebelliousness, sadness, or withdrawal. Hostility and acting-out behaviors may be predictable and "necessary" from certain points of view. (That doesn't mean one should passively accept such behavior.) Be aware of patterns of behavior, of relating, and of development in your children. Ask yourself how they may relate to your behavior. (For example, one executive realized that the onset of bed-wetting in one five-year-old child and of angry temper tantrums in a three-year-old coincided with his being out of town every week for several weeks in a row. Noticing this, he talked about it with his children and his wife and then canceled an upcoming trip. The tantrums and bed-wetting went away within two days.) Most behavioral difficulties with children and adolescents (no matter how dramatic) are transient phenomena.

If things seem different and if they don't add up, consult with your spouse and then speak with your family physician or pediatrician. If what he or she tells you does not settle things, get a consultation with a specialist; it's worth the time and money. Various sources are available for seeking such consultations in your community if your physician cannot help you find someone of quality (see Appendix B).

ALCOHOLISM

Executives are to alcohol as fish are to water. This association may be offensive, but it fits with the popular caricature of the executive. After all, we are portrayed at business luncheons and cocktail parties always with a drink in our hand. Advertisements, particularly those for expensive brand liquors, not infrequently present (and therefore stimulate) the image of an important, prosperous "executive-type" man or woman relaxing with that particular brand. In movies, stories, and novels (and not infrequently in reality), those among us "at the top" are portrayed with small, well-equipped, discreetly disguised bars in our offices. "Relax after work with a drink" could be the motto on the executive coat of arms, at least as far as the popular caricature is concerned. Perhaps this caricature is close to the reality.

> A substantial majority—72 percent—of executives among "Fortune 500" companies with occupational alcoholism programs believe that their organizations have saved money as a result of their companies' programs. A positive assessment of program effectiveness in overcoming job impairment due to alcohol use was almost universal among this group.[16]

Our country is not the only one where alcoholism represents an enormous social problem. I find myself taken aback every time I review the statistics on alcoholism and problem drinking in this country. Given both the caricature and the reality of the executive's association with problem drinking, I am going to share some of these statistics with you.

"Problem drinking" means the taking in of alcohol in such a way that it produces an impairment in physical, mental, or social functioning. Seven percent of the entire population over eighteen years of age in the United States are problem drinkers or alcoholics. (Alcoholism refers to a physical and psychological addiction.) In numbers that figure currently translates into 9 to 10 million adults! These individuals do not quietly sit in a corner with their impaired functioning, having no affect on the family and community systems. Eleven percent of the total deaths in the United States are related to alcohol use and misuse. Problem drinking and alcoholism are estimated to cost this country approximately $43 billion a year (based on 1975 data). A partial breakdown of the details in that figure reveals that $19.6 billion dollars are accounted for by lost production, $12.7 billion by health and medical care costs, and $5.1 billion by motor vehicle accidents.

We shouldn't fool ourselves that alcoholism is an issue confined to younger and older adults. There has been a gradual, documented increase in alcohol use among children and adolescents since World War II. One recent study of seventh through twelfth graders (age twelve through eighteen) indicated that 74 percent of all these children drank alcohol: 79 percent of all the males and 70 percent of all the females. The alcohol intake increased with each succeeding grade.

Problem drinking for the nonadult is defined somewhat differently than for the adult. In the child and teenage population, problem drinking refers to either "drunkenness six or more times in the past 12-month period or the presence of negative consequences from drinking two or more times in at least the last three out of five specific situations during which alcohol was used in the past year, or both."[17] For the nonadult, such negative consequences associated with drinking mean being in trouble with teachers or the principal of the school, being in trouble with friends, driving while under the influence of an excess of alcohol, being criticized by peers for use of alcohol and the behavior associated with it, and being in trouble with the police. At this time, 17 percent of all young people between the ages of fourteen and seventeen years in the United States are considered problem drinkers. This translates into over 3.3 million young people! The trend is toward increasing use and abuse. For example, between 1966 and 1975 the number of young people under eighteen years old reporting that they were intoxicated one or more times each month increased to 19 percent from 10 percent.

Think for just a minute about all that I have just presented. You and I come to the same conclusion: From an economic, social, family, or personal point of view, alcohol abuse is no joke. As executives, people interested in control and understanding, let us review a few more facts about alcoholism. Although often used for social reasons, to increase conviviality and induce relaxation, alcohol in excessive amounts produces anxiety and depression. It is associated with all kinds of physical disease states. Not sufficiently recognized by the public is its very clear association with increased risk for certain kinds of cancer. Its abuse is also clearly associated with suicide, with accidents (of all kinds), with child abuse and neglect, with child molesting, and with domestic (marital) violence. It affects an individual's memory, ability to use his or her intellectual capacities, and ability to control impulses. Only recently recognized are the effects it has on the unborn, the so-called Fetal Alcohol Syndrome. A pregnant mother with an intake of three or more ounces of liquor per day produces this syndrome, which has been discovered as being the third leading cause of birth defects and mental retardation in this country.

We know so much about alcohol abuse, yet it continues to expand as a problem. We know that parental abuse of alcohol very clearly influences children to the extent that it often foreshadows problem drinking in the children. We know that children growing up in homes that are chronically disrupted by domestic strife, homes in which the emotional bonds between parent and child are either seriously weakened or poorly established, have an increased risk of abusing alcohol when they become adults. With specific reference to the statistics given earlier, please note also that we now have correlations over a twenty-five-year period which show that early drinking behavior clearly predicts later-life drinking habits.

Prevention of Alcohol Abuse:
Parents and the Family

How do we deal with the special reality of alcohol abuse within our community and, for some of us, within ourselves? It is both a response to stress and a generator of special stresses. Although common, indeed an increasing problem, alcohol abuse carries with it a heavy stigma: The drinker is marked as being different, somehow unwhole and, hence, unwholesome. Again, stigma serves to inhibit us from even admitting to ourselves that we have the problem for which we are stigmatized. Without admitting the existence of a problem, dealing with it becomes, to say the least, rather difficult. Stigma also allows the family and community to separate themselves from the problem: It is his or her "bag," not ours! In the case of alcohol abuse, nothing could be farther from the truth.

The first step in prevention and intervention is clearly to recognize alcohol abuse as a significant challenge to *all* of us and not just to those who have actual drinking problems or alcoholism within themselves or their immediate family. Much evidence exists that problem drinking is a learned behavior. Certainly, some individuals have greater predisposition to such learned behavior than others. (Indeed, there may be a genetic component to this predisposition.) But I cannot overemphasize the importance of learned behavior. In general, alcohol use and abuse are issues which form part of the educational responsibilities of parents, families, schools, and community organizations.

For parents, the reality of alcohol use relates closely to the challenging responsibilities of the parental role. These responsibilities include teaching our children how to deal with the anxieties, conflicts, and frustrations that life presents. For those who find themselves poorly educated and little experienced in dealing with these dimensions of existence, alcohol smooths the way: It changes one's orientation to time and space, it changes one's orientation to people, it enhances denial and forgetfulness, and it provides an excuse for not coping or not coping terribly well. Ours is a society of great resources; indeed, for those in the socioeconomically privileged groups it appears to offer excess resources and freedom of choice. Despite our socioeconomic advantage, the resources most of us have do put limits on the extent to which we and our children can partake of existing choices and opportunities. We and our children thus experience at various times resultant conflict and frustration. These feelings, if left unattended, can become powerful forces influencing our behaviors. Growing up without internalizing any sense of limits to consumption and self-gratification renders a person dramatically predisposed to these conflicts and frustrations which not infrequently become excuses to ourselves and others for drawing the veil of alcohol between self and reality. Talking to our children about these things, training them to deal constructively with the many teasing realities of life, and teaching them to control consumption and gratification help them in many ways, including reducing the probability of the kind of alcohol abuse which derives from such "tensions."

We know that from the beginning, the paths to prevention and early intervention must be traveled on starting with the family. Studies have documented that children model themselves after parents, including their abuse of alcohol. We have other supporting data. We know that academic achievement and church attendance or some form of regular religious involvement all predispose children and adolescents *against* abuse of alcohol. Parental tolerance (permissiveness) of deviant behavior in children and adolescents predisposes them toward alcohol abuse. We also know that children who grow up alienated from parents and other adult figures are also dissatisfied with themselves; these characteristics together render such children high risks for alcohol abuse. Finally, we can responsibly claim that when frequent drinking and severe intoxication are seen in young people this behavior reflects both individual psychopathology (that is, serious psychological problems) and family pathology. I suggest that you as a parent use this knowledge yourself, within your family and friendship network to develop your own ways of preventing alcohol abuse in your children.

Our children are surrounded by excess, by promises of instant pleasure, by comfort, and by promises of easy solutions. These children have money to spend. They see advertisements in which alcoholic beverages are associated with having a good time and being grown up, mature, financially comfortable, sexually attractive, and socially successful. We use alcohol when we entertain, when we eat, and when we relax. In the junior and senior high schools, alcohol is unofficially everywhere; its consumption is an expression of rebellion, a way to socialize, and a way to be comfortable with oneself and others.

Neither a "witch-hunt" nor prohibition will help. The help lies within ourselves as parents. If the parental role is taken seriously and is enjoyed, bonding between parent and child naturally occurs. This, in turn, leads to role modeling, a powerful force which can either synergize with or resist behaviors observed outside the family. The information and education parents give their children is more readily accepted if the children and parents relate to each other in a caring, sincere, and honest fashion (which includes the permission to disagree and to have strife).

So we return to that first step, a clear delineation of the reality of alcohol as a problem within our society—a problem existing within the school system and within peer groups of both children and adults. We must recognize the stigma created by alcohol abuse and understand how that very stigma reinforces a person's inability to face difficult realities. Finally, caring parents, parents who see the importance of their role, will provide structure and limits for their children. These, they realize, are expressions of caring and love, not the antitheses of caring and love. Engaging these realities is not easy. It takes work, attention, and time.

MOVING

It is fascinating that moving is so common within our society yet so little studied by the behavioral and social science communities. Indeed, there remains a dramatic lack of systematically collected information about the phenomenon of household relocation.

As we all know—and certainly executives know this—our image is that of a mobile society. In part it is related to the great immigrations of people onto the shores of North America over the past three centuries. Individuals and families from various cultures moved in great numbers: English, Northern and Western Europeans, African, Scotch-Irish, Eastern and Southern Europeans, Chinese, Japanese, Mexican, West Indians, and Southeast Asians. Just to remind ourselves of the enormity of this influx of people, recall that between 1900 and 1920, 14.5 million people came to these shores.[18]

Today movement continues, but it takes place primarily within the United States. Most moves actually occur within the same county. Other than migrant farm workers, probably the most mobile group are members of the executive class; they not only account for much of the in-county moving that is done, but they constitute a large number of those who move from one state to another, from one part of the country to another, and from this country to other countries and back. When people move, they tend to move to similar kinds of communities. It is interesting to note that close to 70 percent of the American population lives in what are called "standard metropolitan statistical areas" rather than in "rural areas." (The definitions are based on population density.)

Those who move most—and most frequently among the executive class—tend to be in the twenty-five through forty age range. (Obviously, older members of the executive class also move.) Moves are determined by company or government organization policy. Moves are determined also by individuals as they go from one company to another or from one academic organizational setting to another.

Moving is a major stress. It challenges the individual and the family structure within which he or she resides. It destabilizes the dynamic equilibrium that has been established in one location. This dynamic equilibrium must be restabilized in a new community—something that takes conscious effort and time. At least five major issues are associated with moving. The first has just been mentioned. Second, moving produces a situation in which participants are forced into a relationship of greater dependency upon each other and greater interaction with each other. Third, in moving, one leaves behind the supports as well as the responsibilities represented by friends and family members who do not engage in the move. Fourth, a move produces new stresses as well as an increase in existing stresses; hence, during a move we should all expect to have some symptoms of stress. Fifth, we must engage in certain behaviors as part of our coping with the many ramifications of a move.

We know that moving changes family goals, rhythms, and interactions. We know also that when a move is based on a clearly articulated purpose, that purpose serves as an organizing principle for all involved. It provides structure, a context within which people can assess the resources they have and the tools they will need for coping with the predicted stresses. We know that frequent moves, meaning moves that occur one or more times a year or even once every two years, are very disruptive to individuals and families. We know that the reactions of the parents to the move intimately affect the reactions of the children. Children's reactions, in turn (and the reactions of others), are a function of their age, their understanding of the reasons for the change, and their expectations for their existence after the change.

Each individual in a move has to face a series of realities. The most obvious is that they are leaving a familiar situation for a less familiar or completely unfamiliar one. They are leaving relatives and friends, sometimes intimate ones, for an environment where there will be fewer friends and relatives or perhaps none. They are leaving a community they know well from a physical and social point of view. They are leaving familiar helping resources. Since executive moves usually happen because of the executive's career (this applies as well to the two-executive couple where the motivation for the move would come from one of the two), the other spouse leaves behind some established role or career; the children leave behind established peer communities and familiar schools. For each individual there is uneasiness and anxiety associated with reestablishing familiarity, friends, and networks of acquaintances. Very often, because moves are associated with stress, they produce transient changes in one's physical rhythms or functioning as well as emotional changes. An increase or a decrease in food intake, the appearance of a sleep problem, and/or increased irritability are the usual expressions of these changes, though the details vary with age and personality. All these reactions are basically physiological expressions of increased vigilance in response to the stress.

The issue of fear has greater importance for children and adolescents than for adults. Children are fearful about their ability to accommodate to the change and to meet the various challenges. Such fears and concern over accommodation are experienced differently depending on the age of the child. Preschool children tend to be made anxious by any major environmental change and need a great deal of consistent help in reestablishing some sense of comfort and control. School-age children are less expressive of their difficulties, mourn mostly for the loss of a peer group, but tend to rapidly reintegrate themselves into a new community. Early adolescents have a terribly difficult time leaving established friendship networks and getting themselves accepted into new ones. The middle to late adolescents tend to be resentful and not infrequently express refusal to move; for them, the leaving of peer groups and familiar situations is dramatically anxiety-provoking, tending to push them back into their families and into an uncomfortably dependent relationship on their parents (something they resist as much as the move).

Thus, for all individuals as well as for the family as a unit, there exists a variety of challenges. We all must, in the context of moves, establish new social networks. We must establish a familiarity with the new community and its resources. We must establish or aid each other in establishing peer networks and careers within the new neighborhood, work, and schools. We must work toward regaining a sense of comfort and control with the new situation. In short, one has to work toward the establishment of a feeling of "home."

A Tale of Two Cities

Two major kinds of special situations are related to moving. The first of these involves those circumstances in which all members of the family cannot move together and there is temporary or long-term separation of family members. Perhaps a child stays behind for reasons of schooling. Perhaps a parent and the children stay behind for reasons of economics, difficulty in selling a house, or a spouse's career demands. In some cases the situation produces the phenomenon known as "the commute," where one parent or the other spends much of a week working in one city and comes into his or her "home" community as a transient visitor for long weekends or part of a weekend. Obviously, very special stresses are associated with these situations.

The other special situation involves the overseas move.[19] In both these special situations—overseas moves and separation of family members resulting from the move—families can help themselves by being very clear about the reasons for the particular changes that affect them. They need to be as well prepared as possible, since the normal challenges associated with moving will be heightened in these situations. There is greater probability of social isolation when a family is not together or when it moves overseas. Guilt is engendered and stress becomes greater when the family is not together or when, because of a move abroad, one leaves family, intimate friends, and important others behind. A divided family has difficulty maintaining support and friendship networks. A family transplanted to a different culture and community will need to make extra efforts toward establishing a support and friendship network in the new place.

Overseas moves involve very special problems. These range from the apparently mundane—such as restrictions on the entry of pets or certain kinds of pets into different countries—to the more complex issues of language and cultural differences. (Even this apparently minor issue of whether pets can accompany the family can be of great significance when examined carefully, since pets sometimes play an important role in the dynamics of American families.) Learning a new language, adjusting to the culture within which that language exists, becoming familiar with the economic system of a new community—all challenge the capabilities of even the strongest individuals. For most of us, even when we have talents in other languages, it is tiring to speak and think in a language we have learned after childhood. Also, when one has learned a language after childhood, it is rare to be able to capture the emotional nuances and associations of that language and the culture. True, you can try to see it all as an adventure and even a privilege, but the differences are still there and translate into a chronically heightened state of vigilance. This heightened vigilance is associated not merely with obvious, pragmatic situations such as the greater complexities in dealing with emergencies, but it appears as well in dealing with those everyday situations in which something more than a comfortable reflex response is needed. Finally, the issue of reentry into one's own country and culture after having adjusted to another culture and language needs attention. Reentry is a complex phenomenon and one that is not easily accomplished. It is often particularly difficult for the homemaker and for the teenager. Both must significantly alter their expectations and come to terms with dramatic changes in their support systems.

Coping with Moves

How you cope with moving obviously depends not only on your individual resources and an understanding of the purpose for the change but also on the amount of time you spend planning and preparing for the move and the subsequent process of settling in. When you are going to move, review the purpose of the move with the family: why the move, where the family is moving, and what it is like there. Encourage members of the family to share their reactions (no matter what these reactions are) and to ask questions. Listen attentively and respond, even though it may be hard for you, given the many demands on your time. Your efforts will be well spent. Involve the family in planning and preparing for the move. As parents you have the lead role in planning the move. The quality of your planning and your comfort (your sense of control) is an important statement to the children, and it directly affects their coping behavior. Pay attention also to the process of everyone's disengagement from the community, workplace, and friendship networks. Realize that for all of you there are physical and emotional challenges stimulated by the moving process itself and by the processes of settling in and reestablishing yourselves elsewhere.

Everyone's needs are different. You should, as a parent, recognize this. Be concrete and pragmatic in these situations, so that children understand the move as an exceptional process in which democratic principles are not too helpful; someone must make decisions, take responsibility, and move things along. On the other hand, try to give each child some particular responsibilities. Even the littlest children cope better if they feel they have a role in the move and some thing or things (even if these are simply a stuffed animal or toys) that they are responsible for. Whatever the responsibilities, see that they extend through the period of settling in.

Physiological and emotional changes always go hand in hand with major changes. In your role as parent be aware of any physiological changes or mood states that become chronic or of difficult emotional states that become chronic (even if they do not develop to the point of isolated behavior or disorientation). These need particular attention and sometimes assistance from outside the family, especially if the symptoms last more than six to eight weeks after a move has been completed.

Working together on the move, planning for it, separating from the old home and community, making the transition, and reestablishing yourselves—all these can be strengthening experiences. This will be true for a fair number of people who are psychologically resilient and very adaptable—"survivors," as I call them. My impression, however, is that a fairly large number of individuals who have grown up with frequent moves have found such experiences seriously disrupting. For them, forming intimate relationships with other people is difficult. They are often chronically anxious without knowing why. They are afraid to have feelings of belonging to any place or of making any commitments, and they carry this fear with them for years.

Do not take moving casually. It is a major change. This applies most particularly when the move means leaving a familiar community for a relatively unfamiliar or completely unknown one. Pull your spouse and children together around you during such major changes. By doing so and by attending to the guidelines presented here, you will reduce the possibility of serious adjustment problems for all concerned. If you really "play it right" and have a reasonable amount of good fortune, the family may even gain strength from the experience.

DEATH AND LOSS

A young girl, living in New Orleans: "My grandmother . . . she told me she had lived a nice long life . . . and she was ready to leave us, whenever God decided she had been with us long enough. . . . One day we found her. . . . She was dead. . . . I wanted to go in the room but they wouldn't let me . . . to say goodbye."[20]

The young girl's maid: "She wonders about life, and what it's about, and what the end of things will be. That's good. But she's stopping now. That's what they want: no looking, no staring, no peeking at life. No questions."[21] These two quotes dramatize your responsibilities as a parent to help yourselves and your children relate to death and loss. This means asking certain questions of yourself, encouraging your children to do so, and answering such questions as best you can. Death and loss are natural experiences. How you relate to them transmits an important emotional tone to your children. Your misunderstandings and anxieties about them are transmitted to your children and often contribute to a lowering of their tensile strength. What follows are some general comments which will stimulate further thinking on the subject and which at some point will be of use to you.

Of human experiences, death and loss are among the most

passionate and the most fraught with feeling. They also are truly not separable from each other. Death means a "loss" and "loss" implies a struggle with the continuation of being—hence, with the potential cessation of being. The meaning of both cannot reasonably be generalized on, since the meaning in each instance varies depending on who was involved, how the death or loss happened, how much time there was for preparation (if any), what the surrounding circumstances were, and what relationship all the events had to the developmental stage or age of the various individuals involved.

Death and Loss in the World of Children

About children, certain generalizations are useful. At the age of two to three years, children usually become aware of death through animals, insects, and plants. These are environmental experiences, experiences of seasons and of flora and fauna. Children notice something is different—a moth doesn't fly, or a flower wilts. The child asks why. This is how it begins.

Later, children begin getting explanations from grown-ups and even from other children, and between the ages of four and six years they start to realize that death can apply to people. Only after the age of seven through nine years do children understand death as something that involves them as well, that is not reversible, that they cannot will to be undone.[22]

From the beginning in a child's life, death becomes associated with change, with the loss of at least behaviors and relatedness, as something of memory. It also becomes involved with the child's sense of his ability to control things and the absence of such control. During the years of two through nine, children learn about, develop, and discard rituals of their own while incorporating those of family and community. Thus, rituals (repeated behaviors that organize and structure events), with their psychological and social meanings, become built into the issues of the sense of death and loss, of control and noncontrol.

Deaths of other people known to children *always* affect children. When they react to death with silence, lack of comment, a bland expression, or a few passing tears—these are frequently misinterpreted by adults as indicating minimal awareness or understanding of what has passed. At all ages children are keenly aware of these events. They need help in organizing such experiences, which are as dramatic for them as for grown-ups. In all situations of loss, children need to be encouraged to talk and draw pictures as an additional way of expressing their questions, fears, understandings, and misunderstandings about the event. They need explanations, but most of all they need patient listening.

Various studies indicate that in certain situations more focused efforts are needed by parents and other caretakers. If, for example a mother (not father) is lost prior to the age of eleven years and is never successfully replaced by a new mothering figure, this loss often appears to be associated with depressive disorders in adult life.[23] (This is a statement based on retrospective analysis. It does not mean that all those individuals who experience the loss and lack of replacement of a mother figure will unquestionably have a depressive disorder in their adult life. It does mean that such individuals as a group are particularly vulnerable to depressive disorders.) Both male and female children experiencing loss of either parent and nonsuccessful replacement of that parent during their childhood frequently seem to have much unresolved anger at the loss, which is perpetuated in the form of chronic anger and hostility states in their adult life.

Death and Loss in the World of Adults

"Each person is born to one possession which out-values all others—his last breath."[24] This quotation from Mark Twain illustrates one way we adults deal with death—through humor. For almost all of us in almost all (including extreme) situations, the drive to hold on to existence is extraordinarily powerful. What was supposedly one of Lord Nelson's remarks while dying aboard his ship may seem a bit extreme: "The pain is so great that one might wish oneself dead but one would like to live a little longer, too."[25] However, in over a decade of consulting with physicians about patients who have cancer, with rare exceptions—even in situations of extreme suffering—have I seen an individual willingly give up, seeking death.

Concerning both loss and death, a word caricature of the American attitude might be, "No body, no ritual, no transitions." Nothing could be more antithetical to our realities as human beings than this view, which takes no account of our need to make adjustments when death or loss occurs. Besides being part of life, death and loss are something that live in memory. They are "for always." To pretend otherwise is to undermine one's capacity for dealing with the experience.

There are books and publications available (see Appendix A) as sources for discussion on how to deal with the many special situations of death and loss. Different responses are required, depending on the particular situation and circumstance—whether one is talking about the death of a child or a spouse through suicide or accident, in youth or old age or isolation (to name just a few of the possibilities). However, one can usefully offer certain generalizations relevant to all circumstances.

Coping

Know the responses associated with death and loss. These are the two most challenging experiences for human beings, experiences that remind us of our limited control and of our finite selves. Naturally associated with death and loss are extreme feeling states, which include not only sadness but also anger, guilt, and sometimes fear. The grief and other feelings associated with death and loss are not by any stretch of the imagination abstract psychological processes. They are very physical reactions: Appetite is lost; body rhythms change, particularly with respect to sleep; and even general health status changes transiently.

Know the process of adjustment to loss. Called mourning, it occurs in relationship to lost positions, lost objects, and lost individuals. This adjustment is terminated once there is some form of psychological settling in, some incorporation of the experience, and some perspective achieved on what exactly has been lost. When the loss involves an individual with whom one was close, we tend to incorporate (make part of ourselves) characteristics of that individual as part of the resolution of the mourning process. Indeed, this incorporation of a lost, loved individual is dealt with by a few human societies, such as the Fore of New Guinea, through a ritual cannibalizing of departed family members.[26] Although we are not so concrete in this culture, the need to incorporate and thus somehow attenuate and adjust to the loss is no less real within us. How to arrive at this point is where rituals come in.

Rituals are absolutely necessary. They organize mourning. They even assist in the intellectual process of rationalizing the special event. No matter what our age, rituals help us to set boundaries as we go through the same processes we went through as infants in situations of transient separation; there is a searching, a seeking, and a testing out of the reality of the departure. By not allowing children or ourselves to identify the reality of a loss, by discounting the importance of ritual behaviors during periods of important loss, we interfere significantly, sometimes permanently, with the necessary transition to involvement with life after loss. Other people, sometimes organized groups, help in these processes.

Do not try to protect yourself or your children from what is. Such pretending cannot change reality and it exacts a heavy price from those who do not allow themselves to mourn. Drugs are one readily available aid to such "pretending." The use of tranquilizing and sedating drugs is not helpful (though there are occasional, brief exceptions). Using such drugs impedes the behaviors necessary to individuals of all ages when adjusting to death and loss. The crying is necessary, the sobbing is necessary, the anger is necessary, the transient withdrawal is necessary, and the sadness is necessary.

Be with your community at times of loss. That community is represented by the greater family, by friends, and by acquaintances. It is also represented by the subculture and the culture. From these sources the individuals involved receive the necessary signals concerning their reinvolvement with life and their future orientation. It is from the community that one receives sanctions to end one's mourning.

Much of the preceeding discussion concerning loss in the context of death is applicable to all forms of important loss. For children, parents, and families in today's society, such important losses include things seen as major failures, loss of social or economic status, and job-related removal from one's culture or one's preferred community.

You can prevent dysfunction from following any form of significant loss by attending to the realities of yourself, your children, and the situation. Consider the nature of the loss, as well as the strengths and vulnerabilities you all have. Children know when loss has occurred. You, for your part, should give them permission, indeed should encourage them, to question, to react. Help them to look without fear at the reality of what is, to understand and accept their own reactions. Teach them that sadness and anger are appropriate. Engage them in rituals (whatever yours might be), showing them through your respect and responses the boundaries and comfort that rituals provide. Show them through your example the strength and hope that come from mourning within a family and a community.

OF FAMILIES, FAMILY NETWORKS, AND SELF-HELP GROUPS

Almost every family at some time must face the challenge of dealing with one or more of these special situations. Even so, unless we are in such a situation, we tend to think of them as happening to "them," not to "us." Yet special challenges are part of the reality of our human condition. To illustrate this point let me present only two sets of conditions out of the very many that exist: The first is cancer; the second involves mental health problems. With respect to the former, please recall that four out of every ten people reading this book will develop some form of cancer during their lives. Concerning mental health problems, few bother to recognize that one out of every five of the children and adolescents in your community already has a mental health problem that impairs his or her functioning to the degree that intervention is needed beyond what the family can provide. Special situations are always stigmatizing in some way for the people involved, ridiculous as this is when viewed objectively in the context of the human condition. Much more wholesome attitudes about life would include greater empathy and interest in recognizing and solving problems than in labeling other people "unfortunate" and "defective" and probably beyond our responsibility or ability to help.

Resources for dealing with difficult situations include our selves and our families. But the challenges may be of such an order or complexity that even further resources are needed. This certainly applies to such problems as alcohol abuse, separation and divorce, moving, and death and loss. It also applies to health problems, chronic physical or intellectual or emotional impairments as may be found in any one of us.

Dealing with any of these situations means coping with stress. Effective dealing with stress includes both reducing it and maintaining it within tolerable limits.[27] We know that for individuals, groups, and even social systems, success in coping adds considerably to their sense of worth, of control, and of strength.

Networks

One critical resource for successful coping involves our relationships and interactions with other people: family, relatives, friends, and interested individuals. The more similar the social experiences and cultural and subcultural values of the people involved are, the more those individuals will be able to help one another. Affiliation within kinship or ethnic groups clearly aids group coping. Such acceptance of interdependency seems to free individuals to be more flexible and better able to find solutions or to accept what can't be changed. The feedback individuals get by interacting with others in group settings enhances their capacity to anticipate the future. Such predictability is critical in all stress situations. Predictability or a sense, even an illusion, of it provides continued awareness of one's potential for control and makes one more effective in dealing with stress.

During much of what I have discussed I have emphasized the need for individuals to relate to each other. We must recognize, however, that such relating, as it occurs, leaves much to be desired. Our open-ended, complex society requires more relating than we actually do within families. One study, for example, concluded "that the average unit—husband, wife, and two children—spend only 26 minutes each week in intimate conversation."[28] As it turns out, the busyness of families and individuals mostly involves the mechanics of life. It has rarely been otherwise. Yet perhaps today, given the complexity of our civilization and the extent of stress and uncertainty, things should change. Perhaps there is a great need for more time spent in intimate conversation.

Well, where does one turn beyond one's self and one's family in times of special stress? Most of us turn to books (such as those presented in Appendix A), we turn to friends and family, we turn to clergy, we turn to professionals, and we turn to helping groups (see Appendix B).

Professionals clearly represent a special resource. The best of my kind serve as a critical pool of knowledge, a resource of specialized experience, and a source of nonjudgmental understanding of fellow human beings. Yet we have limitations, particularly when it comes to dealing with the environment, the community, and stigma. Other resources are needed for dealing with these.

Extenders of Self and Community

I will close this chapter by encouraging you the executive to think about "natural person-to-person supports."[29] These mutual support groups are a very special resource. Sociologically, they are an extension of the healthy family, in which mutuality and reciprocity predominate.[30]

Mutual help and support systems—known as self-help groups—have proliferated over the past twenty years and continue to do so. There is little general public recognition of their importance and activity. They seem to be a natural development in the country that was once described by Alexis de Tocqueville as a "nation of joiners."

Studied for many years at the Harvard University Laboratory of Community Psychiatry, these groups are best described as peers helping each other, based on personal experience and a sharing of needs and burdens.[31] Such groups allow a crossing of normal social, economic, and disciplinary boundaries. They involve themselves with the important, immediate needs of the individuals, families, or groups who form them, and they provide immediate, pragmatic assistance. The variety of such groups is extraordinary.

What follows is a partial listing presented simply to provide a sense of the variety of such organizations; each one may have dozens or even hundreds of branches, and a few have spread beyond the borders of the United States. The list includes Alcoholics Anonymous, Al-Anon, the Candlelighters, Gamblers

Anonymous, Little People of America, Make Today Count, the Mended Hearts (people who have had open-heart surgery), Ostomy clubs (people who have had their colons removed and live with functioning ileostomies or colostomies), Parents Without Partners, LaLeche League (breast-feeding organization), Reach for Recovery (women who have had mastectomies), Recovery Incorporated (people who have been hospitalized in mental institutions), and TOPS, or Take Off Pounds Sensibly. This partial listing of self-help groups does not include organizations that have developed with partial formal affiliation with establishment organizations; examples are the hot lines students have with their colleges or universities or other community efforts in affiliation with religious and fraternal organizations. All these self-help groups and networks seek to foster the autonomy of the individuals who join them through the interactions of the members. The individuals come from all parts of a community and all walks of life. Thus, the term *network* is truly appropriate. Individuals can move from one part of the United States to another and find sister organizations in their new communities, thus providing a certain kind of stability within such networks. Mutual help groups, by the nature of the interactions within them, allow both for ventilation and the reduction of feelings of isolation. They also tend to be problem-oriented, interested in laying out strategies for coping with the particular problems they have formed to discuss. This problem orientation goes beyond symptoms to actually dealing with social issues such as stigma, economic problems, communication problems with the family. Because the groups are made up of peers, the interactions tend to reinforce, even validate, the identity of individuals. They provide a context in which emotional mastery can be attained and are particularly effective in helping to counteract situations in which an individual has a lowered self-esteem due to illness, chronic physical condition, loss of a body part, obesity, accident, loss of employment, loss of a loved one, or any of a variety of other situations. Such groups, when formed by the individuals involved, are helpful to participants of almost all ages. (One group has even been formed by teenagers based on their distress at parental divorce.[32])

Great strength comes through mutual support groups. They

provide a safe ground for ventilation, and reality testing, a forum for seeking of advice, and a potential resource for friendships and community assistance. They are a considerable resource in our armamentarium for dealing with stress, particularly with unusual stress. They provide dimensions of community that cannot be provided by traditional healers. I commend your attention to such groups or the potential that exists in forming them, whether the place and reasons involve issues of work, coping with a new culture, separation and divorce, or illness.

6

The Executive—
The Parent

Many corporations are expressing deep concern these days about what they see as a pull between family life and child rearing on the one hand and the functioning of high-level executives on the other. The apparent conflict is not confined to corporation life; it is felt in all areas of the public and private sectors—wherever men and women work to "maintain a system of cooperative effort." Though sincerely felt, the concern of the corporations is based on a dramatic misperception of human realities. Dedicated, hard work and joyful, intense family life are not by any means contradictory.

The misperception itself highlights the obvious need in today's culture for people to have special training in setting priorities and balancing their energies. Such training is particularly helpful for career-oriented individuals whose work is coupled with family life and child rearing. Indeed, executives who live in families and bring up children can learn to handle these activities in such a way that rather than taking away from their careers and energies, family life and child rearing add tremendously to energy, creativity, and tensile strength in all areas of their lives.

You recall my saying earlier that parenting is an executive role and that the majority of executives are parents. The abilities that you have as a well-functioning executive give you tremendous capacities and strengths which can be used in the parent role. Similarly, the experiences you have as a parent and from existence within a family add tremendously to your career capacities.

I make these statements with confidence, despite the evidence of unnecessary (avoidable) dysfunction and pain in a great many executive families. That dysfunction and pain clearly are associated with the demands of the executive role and with the coping strategies traditionally employed to deal with those demands. There is a certain irony in these dysfunctions: the disaffections and chronic misunderstandings within the families, the running away of the children, the separations and divorces, and the alcoholism and drug abuse. The irony arises because of the resources that are available to executive families: their socioeconomic level, their intellect, the education available to them, and the particular abilities of both executives and the individuals they tend to marry. All these resources theoretically should render executives and executive families stronger, healthier, and more "together" than other families.

You as an executive can improve the situation for yourself and your colleagues. You can do so by deliberately examining "the executive–the parent" and determining how the two are bound into one another and how you can act to enhance them both. That is the form and substance of this last chapter.

A necessary prelude to this exploration involves the following brief review of the obvious. As executives, our work lives are very much occupied by systems theory in one form or another (though unfortunately, few of us carry the systems view of reality beyond the workplace). The relevant systems theory is referred to by biologists and by those behavioral scientists who have adopted the concept as an ecological approach. When we apply it to human systems, we see immediately the obvious importance that *all* roles and functions, as well as the settings within which they occur, have for each other. Some of the realities I am referring to include:

- Our health and moods affect our work.
- Our work affects our health and moods.
- Career ambitions (a complex subject in and of itself) affect the work we select and our performance in that work.
- Both work and performance affect career ambition.
- Personal life, no matter how disciplined we are or think we are, affects our health, attitudes, moods, and behavior. Hence, it affects our immediate functioning in our workplaces and over time within our careers.
- These careers and workplaces influence our behaviors and moods and the quality of functioning in our private lives. Just think of the above examples—or others—in terms of your own experience. Quite quickly you will think of incidences and illustrations for these examples in your own lives. These interactions are not merely logical and intuitive; they are real. Understanding them is essential to dealing successfully with the reality of being "the executive–the parent" (this includes finding pleasure in both roles). The roles are indeed complex. The interactions between and within them also are complex. Yet the systems approach has symmetry as well as identifiable components; hence, it can be mastered.

You may wonder whether or not you are functioning as a competent executive parent. Even if you are, can you go beyond mere competency? In these final pages, we will review the questions from two points of view: the effects of your work on the family and parenting, and the effects of the family and parenting on your work. The examples offered in this review will provide sufficient models for you, as needs arise, to enhance your own functioning in other dimensions of the executive-parent system.

WORK AS IT AFFECTS THE FAMILY AND PARENTING

Reentry

An executive returns home from work—tense, muscles screaming complaints of abuse—yet aware only of a dull fatigue, numbness, and a deep but vague, nondirected irritability. What does that executive want? A drink? Some quiet? No demands, at least for a little while? Possibly all of those. But the family is glad to see him; they all have things to share and affection to give; they need reactions, and they want attention. Can he handle all that on his "reentry" each night? Or then again, you might rarely return home in the mood described above but you may have things you want to talk about and things you want to or must do. However it may be with *you*, the needs of your spouse and children generally remain the same.

Returning home each night is a significant enough transition to deserve the label of "reentry." Perhaps ideally one should begin the shift on leaving the office. Yet few of us executives function that way; we are often still working in one part of our "heads" as we travel home. If we fail to recognize reentry as a real issue or fail to deal with it despite our awareness of it, our return home becomes a setup for misunderstandings, resentment, anger, and even for hurtful behavior on everyone's part. Think of those times you experienced any one or all of these negative occurrences and felt quite bewildered about what went wrong and why everyone was in such a foul mood.

Accept that the return home at night is a "big deal." Though quiet and often repeated, it still represents one of the day's major shifts within the daily cycle of families. New exchanges and redirections of information, attention, and energy occur. Recognizing it as such allows us to step back and to look at our needs and those of others involved. There should be at this moment a rapid exchange of signals of interest and caring. Most of us do this: We kiss and/or hug, say hello, and ask how was your day. We expect to be kissed and hugged back and asked about our day. If we are not, we feel that something is not right; the stage is thus set for a possible movement of all subsequent interactions towards negative occurrences (a fight, great irritability, etc.).

Knowing the importance of reentry, you should make efforts consciously to begin the shift of interest to family as soon as you leave the office. (There are times, of course, when this is not reasonable to ask of oneself.) Then try frankly and unashamedly to get in touch with your own needs, so that you can communicate them comfortably to your family. For example, after greeting (and do greet!) everyone and after asking about their day, it is important to be able to say, "Let me hear more later. I've had a really difficult day. Let me be alone for a bit while I wash my face and change clothes." Being able to make your needs clearly known helps to reduce miscommunication and misunderstanding. Knowing that you can communicate in this way heightens your sense of control. (Obviously, if someone in the family is in a crisis or emergency situation, you will put aside your needs until that situation has passed.) As a result, you are more predisposed to communicate, to listen, and to respond in terms of *their* needs. In the evening some "breathing space" usually is needed by everyone during the executive's reentry to home. This allows many things to happen quickly and quietly; that is, it allows the necessary shifts to occur in relationships and expectations. For example, with father returning home, children shift their attention to father from each other and mother.

Try, if you are not already doing so, to practice the approach to reentry that I have described. It will quickly become less self-conscious; it will also improve the homecomings.

Refuge

As executives we place considerable pressure on ourselves as well as on those we supervise. Accomplishments, measured differently depending upon one's area of endeavor, are considered "output" and measurements of success. We tend to strive for influence and power and increased resources. To be effective, we need skill in relating to people individually and in groups. This includes mastery of those individual and group behaviors we call workplace politics and power struggles. In many settings it includes the capacity to encourage people to function with interest and effectiveness in their work. To do our jobs, many of us have to travel, sometimes frequently and sometimes on trips of a week's duration or longer. Some of us move from one community to another, either on our own initiative (because of new opportunities) or because the organization is widely dispersed and has determined that for its needs we must move. Many peripheral but important demands form part of our work: We attend social functions and business entertainments; we go to evening and weekend workshops to satisfy some educational needs. The pace of all this combined, even without the predictable and "predictably unpredictable" crash efforts, demands extraordinary energy. Rarely do we feel in control of our time.

We seek refreshment, replenishment of ourselves from the demands made upon us in these various ways. We have exercise —swimming, squash, jogging, tennis, and golf—and the rituals that accompany exercise. Some of us have card games (bridge or poker or the like), chess, gambling, reading, music, or theater. But most executives are alike in that they have families and see them as a special refuge.

"Home Sweet Home," that overused bit of Americana, is still found in souvenir shops emblazoned on plastic plaques with gaudy letters or in so-called country stores as neatly framed pieces of needlework. Overused, but no more trite than the American flag, this phrase expresses our culture's belief in the home as a refuge. Our mythology of home makes it an oasis for physical and spiritual replenishment. At home we relax. At home we are protected from strife. At home there is certainty.

These culturally conveyed expectations of home are a tall order to fill! There is enough truth in them to maintain the myth. After all, the household and the family within it should always be capable of providing refuge and nourishment to the body and spirit. But fulfilling such purposes is not the same as the home and family taking on these purposes as their *primary identity*. The latter, when it occurs, imposes severe constraints on the family and on all of its members. What does one do then with the normal tensions and strife that intrude from outside the home? And with those that naturally develop within the home? If the American myth of "Home Sweet Home" is embraced literally, imposing upon home the *primary identity* of refuge, father, mother, and children—all work toward suppressing the acknowledgment of stresses. Any conflict generates silent discomfort, anxiety, and guilt. Little can be shared or examined except the "safest," most mundane events. Values and ideas cannot be tested. Silence reigns as all pour energy into keeping the misunderstood idea of refuge intact. These attempts seem to work in many families. They work until the pressure has built to such a degree that individual members are pushed into silently developing such dysfunctions as alcoholism or explosive acting out (vandalism or running away) or a complete loss of feelings and mutual respect between two previously caring individuals.

I daresay that what I have just described is the "norm" for all too many executive families. You can be different. Home and family can and should be a refuge. The key is simply to modify your understanding of refuge, of "oasis." A lack of stress and struggle is far from the reality of existence and is synonymous with death. The need for refuge which we all have (and must indulge) comes from a need to limit input, to have clear boundaries, and to refine or regain some sense of direction and control. Some sense of control is paramount. Thus, a refuge, an oasis, is a special place where, buffered from insistent outside demands, we can regain our sense of perspective, of up and down. It is a place where we can regain some sense of control and of potential for more control and thereby reduce our tension. The reality of ourselves and our times is such that sometimes we need that refuge as a "screaming room." Always that refuge must be a place where the expression of pain, struggle, excitement, and anger is permitted but into which only selectively permitted intrusions of the outside world are allowed.

Ask yourselves how many evenings at home you have. Ask yourselves about those evenings. Is there time when family members can be together, to interact as a group or as subgroups without other intrusions? Or are those evenings when you are home punctuated by meals which might be described as fast-paced "incorporations of nourishment." And after meals, do phones ring constantly? Are you driven to call this person and that? Must you and your spouse rush off to this community meeting or that? Does the television corral you all into its mesmerizing arms? Are weekends similar in pattern? If so, you are misusing your refuge. You are also neglecting that other system you are responsible for helping to manage and lead—the family —to a degree that would get you fired from your corporation, foundation, agency, or institution if you were to display similar inattention and nonvigilance on the job.

Accept, then, that when you return home you need a change of pace, rhythm, and input. This need is a biological and neurophysiological reality. The quality of output of the most brilliant and energetic individual decays dramatically when he or she does not allow for any such changes. Not only does the quality of their output suffer, but some eventually will become frankly ill—physically or mentally or both.

The family must be aware of and want to meet those needs. They have similar needs for refuge themselves, whether their "world of work" is finger painting and clambering on jungle gyms, going to classes and competing socially as well as academically, working another job, or managing both household and children. When these needs are not recognized and respected, everyone grows apart. Then—as I sadly hear all too often—the players ask, Why are we no longer together? Why do we no longer understand each other?

The Mormons, I believe, have a ritualized evening time during which the family comes together and outside demands are not allowed. Such a ritual is an absolute necessity in developed countries; it is sorely missed in executive families. Unless the time is ritualized so that outside interferences are not permitted (this includes television), that time will evaporate and will never seem possible. You should choose, based on your own style and that of your spouse and your family, the form that "ritualization" should take. Part of it should be a "buffer time," when the executive who is returning home, or anyone else if they wish, can be alone for a bit—even if simply to wash up and change clothes. Part of it should be, if not a "show-and-tell" time, at least a listening time. Part of it should be a helping time, when help can be requested and given; this can also mean simply listening and advising, teaching, or sharing in someone else's experiences and feelings.

The style and details of refuge time will and should vary from family to family. They will and must over time vary within each family. We age, careers evolve, and children go from toddler-hood to young adulthood; it is all an exciting, ever changing kaleidoscope. I honestly cannot prescribe any more for you except to say that refuge is essential. It exists within the family and the home, but it should not be understood as the primary purpose of either. Honor that refuge by creating within it filters to the outside world that you and others in the family will be able to control. Honor that refuge and thus yourself and the family by making some time every week when outside intrusion is firmly shut off and you can be available to one another. If you follow this prescription, you will feel better, be stronger, and perform better; life will feel better. And there will be fewer unplanned surprises within the family system.

Careerism

Deep investment of self in one's career—"careerism"—gets much approval in our culture. For many individuals it leads to an acceptance in their lives of input overload and work-related rituals such as entertainment and other public behaviors. These individuals find their reference points in their work. The executive's organization serves as the reservoir and conveyor of values. This, in turn, colors the family, sometimes setting up a work-family antagonism. Behaviors and interests follow from what is accepted or even valued by the culture of the workplace. Work overwhelms family, dictating even the executive's approach to parenting.

What I have just described need not be everyone's reality. When I speak of "careerism," I am referring simply to the intense involvement that any one of us can have with our career. All sorts of "baggage" accompanies that intense involvement, including that particular mobilization of physical and psychological energies called ambition. The baggage also contains parcels labeled selective attention, selective inattention, relationship building, skill building, and reputation building. People involved with careerism want to achieve as much success (however they may define it) as they possibly can in their field of endeavor.

I agree with Michael Maccoby's observation that for executives such success means having "an impact on the corporation" or institution.[1] However, the corporate executives Maccoby studied may not represent all executives in our society. Certainly the "constant anxiety" to which Maccoby refers is not, in my experience, a necessary element of careerism.[2] Although many career-oriented executives do get trapped into the definition of success promoted by the system in which they work, many are much freer, generating within the network of their family and friends their own sense of success.

Intense career orientation can be destructive to family and parenting. It can also enrich (and I don't simply mean in dollars!) family and parenting roles. Let us consider it from the positive perspective.

Careerism fits comfortably within society in the United States. For us, "Even the multimillionaire is expected to perform some kind of work. . . . Work is 'good.' . . . It is even believed that the top leaders of industry, government and science work harder than anyone else."[3] Careerism is complex, however. Besides involving the activities already referred to— activities that become enormous sinks for energy and attention —careerism poses additional challenges. It means living in a certain milieu and attaining a certain quality of life, particularly concerning how time is spent and what material goods are used. Also, given the goals that are sought, careerism increases the stakes of normal risks. Work-associated disappointments—the loss of a power struggle; the breaking of an established pace in advancement; or failure to achieve recognition through advancement, promotion, or awards—become major challenges to self-esteem. In the wake of such disappointments come feelings of confusion and even disorientation, as well as doubts and depression. At such times the executive has to regroup his or her resources and cope with the depression and disappointment, while reevaluating himself or herself and the total situation. Dealing with such experiences and isolation is a major trial. Dealing with them with the assistance and support of family and spouse remains a trial but one in which there is considerable loading of the dice in the direction of success.

Careerism need not be destructive to family life. Careerism clearly receives admiration from the greater culture; it is also an expected behavior of people such as executives and professionals who engage in certain kinds of work.

Careerism can be integrated with the family in two ways: clarifying values and developing a perspective on one's existence. First, working out one's system of values. All of us have the responsibility to work out for ourselves whether we like and enjoy children, believe we will enjoy parenting, and see children as important to us in particular and to the society at large. Today it is accepted that legitimate life-styles besides parenting exist for couples. Indeed, a new organization has formed, The Coalition for Operational Parenthood, whose expressed purpose is "to help people make personally effective decisions to be or not to be a parent."[4] Today, at least for those of the executive class, it is irresponsible to have children out of idle interest or reflex. Similarly, it is irresponsible to form a family if doing so is not important to you as an individual. If Maccoby's studies of corporation executives can be extrapolated to all executives— "The main goals stated by all corporate types are a comfortable and protected family life. . . ."[5]—then most of you have already determined what is most important to you. I would simply suggest that you review them to test out whether they are truly embraced by you or simply assumed.

The second action for integrating family and career goals involves establishing your own perspective on your existence. Obviously, reference must be made to what you value and what you believe is important. This action sounds simple, but it isn't.

The hierarchical nature of our society and of the systems within it programs into people a sort of executive "monkey grooming" behavior. We display and participate in this behavior, regardless of whether we are a corporate executive, senior foundation official, professor or dean, or cabinet officer. We need the feedback we get from the system—especially if selectively attended to—to tell us how important we are. From an objective point of view concern about our importance is of course poppycock. All of us have the same ultimate physical limitations, and few of us, no matter how august, leave much behind besides bones and memories for a few people who will eventually follow in our footsteps anyway.

Do not dismiss what I have said simply as morbid realism. It is stated to emphasize our need for stepping back to look at ourselves. Stepping back is a necessary, humbling bit of reality testing which we all should do either on our own or through our religion or both. It is not comfortable or easy or even comforting to do. But unless we make this effort, a perspective on our careers, families, and children, as well as on our own existences, will always elude us.

The purpose of such a perspective is to attain some genuine personal control over the channeling of our energies and spirit. Without such personal control, the immediate demands of the career and material system will (like the "bogeyman") get us every time. The years will spin by and at middle or old age we will wonder what happened and why. Workplaces and careers have only as much soul as we put into them. They are otherwise heartless consumers of time, attention, and energy. They only say "No" or "Enough" when they have broken down. To stay on top of our lives we must set limits; we must manage and control our time and dole out our energy and our attention. Clarifying values and working on perspective are two major tools for attaining such control. However, the greatest tool, indeed the greatest ally we have, is the family.

Family and parenting, given their importance to individual and social systems, counterbalance work and careerism. Within the family, as well as through the work of parenting, we get additional perspectives on ourselves and our community. From interactions with families we also get the most honest feedback as to how well we are maintaining perspective and living up to our values.

As an executive, remember to share with your family the highlights of your work: the ambitions, triumphs, falterings, and even the failures. Let them be aware of some of your activities and skills. Let them know that part of you that uses those skills and engages in those activities. When you have to make special investments of energy and time in your work, make sure that they are time-limited, that the family understands those time limits. Enlist the family's support during such periods. It may involve their having to function generously on a single-parent basis for a while. It may involve their simply supporting you during a difficult work period by decreasing their demands and expectations and by assuaging as much as possible any guilt you may have.

As an executive, do your best not to impose your career on your family any more than you and they decide is necessary and acceptable. Together you must set the limits of the work world, be these limits about moving, the right schools or neighborhood, whom to socialize with, whom to entertain, whether or not to vacation, or how much work to allow on a regular basis over weekends.

Listen to your family. Learn their reactions to what you do, their ideas about your work. Make time to learn how they are developing—and this includes your spouse—and where the changes are leading them; keep current with these things and consider how they relate to your careerism.

Listen to your colleagues and to yourself. Step back sometimes—take a fishing trip, a long walk, or any step back—to see if you've gotten yourself into a "squirrel cage" without noticing it. This can happen to any one of us who is intensely career-oriented. The saving trick is to notice what has happened and to mobilize the energy you need to jump out of the cage.

If you attend to the above, careerism can help make your life an exciting, rewarding one. It can add an extra sense of human meaning to your existence. It can be a source of pride to both you and your family.

Workaholism

According to Michael Radetsky, M.D.: "The stresses due to extravagant expectations and unremitting work are themselves a hazard. However, there is a more insidious process and one more worrisome than mere stress: the erosion of our capacity for wonder, human sharing, and growth of spirit."[6]

Workaholism is probably the worst disease of executives, yet it does not have to be a synonym for executive. Anyone who puts so much time and emotional involvement into their job that other potential realities are blocked out is suffering from a clear case of workaholism. The workaholic is like the horse or mule who has blinders put on it so that it will remain harnessed and plodding in circles as it turns a millstone or water pump. The workaholic is blinded either by a dramatic misperception of his or her job role and importance or by a dramatic misunderstanding of human existence—sometimes by all these factors together. Unfortunately, in some corporate and community environments workaholism is much promoted, is made part of the competitive pressures, and is even begrudgingly admired.

Among ambitious and successful careerists, workaholism appears a predictable, repeated, and yet not a continuous phenomenon. It goes in waves and cycles; clear breaks occur. The comments that follow are relevant to workaholism associated with careerism, but they are written especially about the individual who falls at the extreme end of the spectrum. This extreme end is defined as intense, excessive time involvement with work, which becomes a continuous, uninterrupted process. When such situations are examined, the motivations behind them usually bear no relationship to the criticalness or importance of the work being performed. Rather, they are indications that the individual has lost control for some reason and has been caught up by the process of his or her work. Actual work efficiency often becomes low, quality of output is poor, and the capacity to set priorities has degenerated, with all things getting almost equal attention and receiving almost equal energy. Such individuals undermine not only their own health but also that of their families and even their organization.

You know that you are falling into workaholism when the periods of intense, extra work run one into the other. You become a shadow figure at home. You find yourself traveling more than everyone else and find yourself in the office before and/or after everyone else. The highs and lows of work tend to smooth out. Issues and problems tend to blur. Relaxing or "coming down" from being at work even when away from it never quite happens.

The effects of workaholism are dramatic. Unlike dedicated, hard work that usually receives admiration (as well as resentment), the extreme forms of workaholism raise questions about an individual's ability to be more than simply a hard-working staff person or expendable manager. Extreme workaholism undermines physical health through a combination of inadequate rest and sleep, lack of exercise, and often poor diet, including an excess of caffeine from either tea or coffee. Family life suffers dramatically. There is alienation between family members and resentment of the withdrawal and nonparticipation; com-

munication ceases or is dramatically distortcd. Parcnting suffers, with particularly sad results for young children, who may
grow up with poor self-images and a higher probability of psy-
chosomatjc and emotional disorders if they are shut out emotionally for months and years by a work-addicted parent.[7]

What can one do about the extreme form of work involvement? As always, the obvious step must be taken first: notice
what is going on, what is happening. Family, friends, and colleagues have probably been giving you lots of hints for some
time. The next step involves trying to figure out why you have
slipped into workaholism. Some of the reasons an individual
does this include the following:

- An input overload at work (not an unusual phenomenon),
  upsetting the individual's normal internal system of checks
  and balances (he loses his sense of values and perspective)
  and the family's system of checks and balances (it fails to
  insist on attention and time or it adopts the careerist parent's
  goals too literally).
- A panic reaction to things not going well at work, to feeling or
  knowing things are out of control, to not coping and yet not
  knowing how to regain control or deal with anxiety.
- An escape from nonwork issues that have an even higher
  potential for stress (marital problems, chronic illness of someone in the family, or family problems of other kinds).
- A feeling of anomie, of having no importance and no existence without work (a distorted incorporation of a message
  that our society does indeed broadcast).

As usual, recognizing and trying to define the problem gets
you more than halfway down the path toward successful intervention. Breaking out of workaholism requires you to work on
the problem with yourself, your spouse, your family, key
friends, and trusted associates—your entire support network.
This work will be needed if you are to achieve equilibrium in
your work and private life. The basic reason why you fell into
workaholism must be defined before you can regain control of
your life. Individual psychotherapy or marital and family counseling are frequently helpful. If workaholism has lasted longer

than six to ten months, such professional interventions are almost always necessary to bring about meaningful changes.

Travel

Executive positions today demand some travel. Even though travel is faster and safer than at any time in the past, it does affect family life and parenting. With one parent away, interactions change and roles are modified. A real but usually low level of tension and anxiety always surrounds the trips. These feelings are frequently disguised under practical asides such as "Remember that I now have an automatic travel insurance policy" or "Hi, I'm phoning before I board the plane because I just wanted to tell you that the car is in Lot C, space 241." If your children are toddlers, preschoolers, or in the early school grades, they will be anxious (each age shows anxiety in different ways) and unhappy about any trip, whether for one night or longer. Their anxiety does not decrease with the frequency of your travel; rather, they get trained into how to respond and how to conceal their feelings.

I am not aware of any good studies relating the frequency of travel to the necessity and importance of the business conducted. My observations and hence my current opinion about business travel is this: (1) that some of everyone's business travel could have been handled (often just as well) without the trip and (2) that at least a good 20 percent of executives use travel as a means of getting away from their office routine and home responsibilities. We all owe it to our organizations, our families, and ourselves to continuously evaluate our travel schedules.

Since most of us value our families, spouses, and children, how do we show it at those times when we must leave home? It can be done quite simply. Always share with the family what it is you are going to do and where you are going. Give them, spouse and children, a chance to ask questions about your trip. They should know how long you will be away. But with very young children (at least through age five years) keep the news of your impending trip back until a day or two before you leave. Knowing you will be gone does not help them prepare for it; it only gives them several extra days of anxiety about your being gone and about whether or not you will come back. Your spouse should always have an itinerary with schedule (if by public transportation), locations, and phone numbers. You should review with him or her any issues of family or children that may need attention while you are gone, even if the trip is only two to three days. You should make a commitment to yourself and your spouse that despite being absent you remain involved with the family. This commitment includes making yourself traceable and phoning in once a day. Even on a foreign trip you can still phone in from most countries and should do so once every several days. I'm amazed at the executives who balk at the expense of this—really quite minor—yet who casually drop fifty dollars on drinks with meaningless associates or in a nightclub during lonely evenings. Phone time can be poignant if the trip is a long one, but in all situations it is a concrete expression of caring. Just as importantly and more pragmatically, it allows you to participate in family and parenting issues, including discipline, while you are away. For the young child in particular, the voice contact is important.

Airport gift shops thrive on minitoys and souvenirs for guilty business travelers to bring home to their little ones. Occasional gifts are appropriate and give pleasure, but they should not be associated with your traveling. They soon become expected by the children and hence meaningless. It is much better to always bring back things that help you share the places you have been to: seashells or a stone you have found, a postcard photo of something you enjoyed, an unusual piece of hotel stationery (hard to find these days), or, best of all, some stories about what you did or the people—even interesting or unusual strangers—you saw.

One other suggestion on travel concerns reentry. Not infrequently, on returning home from a trip, you will be tired, perhaps tense, and expecting and needing an interested, attentive welcome. Prepare yourself for what could be a quite different kind of reception. Excited children may have so much to say that their greeting feels more like an assault. Little preschoolers may be angry at your having left them; they may either sulk at your return or greet you enthusiastically and follow that for the rest of the day with behavior that makes Dennis the Menace seem like an angel. You may return by chance at a moment when spouse or others are caught up in some other events or even in a television show or novel. A show of nonchalance on your return may be a mild expression of displeasure at your having been away; as such, it should be considered an acceptable part of reentry and indeed acceptable behavior by those you have left. Remember that existence for them, the routine, went on as usual while you were off to other places. You may feel that you worked hard while away and that being away was a deprivation. They, for their part, may feel that you were off doing different and therefore exciting things and that their staying home was a deprivation. On returning home, everyone must give everyone else a chance to get back their equilibrium.

Although we act casual about travel, it really does make important changes in family rhythms, anxieties, and interactions. By talking with spouse and children you can work out a series of behaviors within your own family that will assist in the accommodation and reentry process. Just be sure that you work these things out together. Also, if you are going to be away for long, encourage family members to do things that will make them feel less uneasy in your absence. They should know that they can get in touch with you if you are needed, but they should also feel free to do such things as go out for simple dinners or other such treats. In these ways, you can lessen the forces that build up resentment while you are away.

FAMILY AND PARENTING: THEIR EFFECTS ON WORK

My clinical experience strongly supports the findings of one social science researcher who stated in 1976 that "The work-family boundary is relevant to organizational effectiveness as well as to family stability. . . it is not a subject an organization should consider simply for the sake of the families."[8] Indeed, as part of the advocacy theme for children and families in this book, I wish to emphasize and reemphasize my observations that parents who are willingly and joyfully involved in parenting are the basis of strong families, individuals who in turn transmit their strength to the community (including the workplace). Let us review again the parent-family role and then talk about accommodating to its effects on the work role.

Of Self as Parent

Theodore Lidz states, "The common desire of American parents is to wish their children to have opportunities that were not available to them; and to become more significant, more learned, more prestigious, happier or wealthier than they have been; and the belief in the malleability of mankind through better techniques as combined with such hopes to make parenthood a self-conscious activity."[9]

This self-consciousness and belief in the malleability of mankind received a major stimulus from Jean Jacques Rousseau's *Emile,* published in 1762. Since the eighteenth century, the combined activities of behavioral and social scientists, educators, and governments have somehow endowed our culture with the belief that "right ways" of parenting exist. Such an expectation in the American mind (which has a certain fondness for formulas) has produced a most unfortunate self-consciousness about parenting. For many, the result of these expectations is that nurturing instincts, feelings, and behaviors are controlled by intellect. The richness of parenting becomes obscured by "methods"; the joys of parenting become restrained and less available.

It may help some of us to recapture spontaneity if we simply identify the expectations we have of ourselves as parents. If mnemonics appeals to you, *DAFNE* will serve to encapsulate these basic expectations:

D   Discipline
A   Availability
F   Flexibility
N   Nurturance
E   Education

Assuming that we have children because we are fond of them (they elicit our capacities for love and empathy), we find also that they provide us with a sense of continuity beyond our immediate selves. What we expect of ourselves as parents is the raising of our children. Besides loving them, we expect of ourselves certain virtuous capacities: to postpone gratification, to compromise, to draw upon extra energy reserves, and to show the self-discipline needed to engage in all these behaviors.

With respect to the children, we expect to make them part of our culture and social system, channeling their energies and behaviors. This is accomplished through discipline and limit setting. At the different developmental stages of children, we expect to be available to them, within reason, in response to their needs. No occupation demands greater flexibility than parenting; we cannot predict illnesses, mood swings, accidents, and sudden urgent (or not-so-urgent) needs. Nurturance, the most basic expectation and, indeed, a genetically programmed activity, refers to all those fundamentals of physical, material, and emotional caring without which none of us can develop. Educating children is an expectation of parents in all cultures throughout human history: teaching what is safe and what is not, teaching how to hunt or hoe, and teaching how to weave or write. Together, they form a simple checklist: If you are providing all elements of DAFNE as a parent and if in doing so the efforts *feel right* (with moments of laughter and joy, as well as of tears), the probability is extraordinarily high that you are doing a fine job.

Coping With Normal Demands

Do you realize that during the week we executives have available to us for direct contact with our families *at the most* something less than one third of our waking hours? Most of those hours are actually spent in the home, yet very little of that time is given to intense, focused interactions with children and spouse. Thus, when more time is needed for focused interactions, we have to take it very deliberately from somewhere else; that "somewhere" is often our work time.

Quite a lot of parenting and "maintenance-of-couple" activities must be engaged in during those few available hours. These activities, which we tend to pursue automatically, include all the sharing, exchanging, caring, and loving we must do to keep active that special relationship called a marriage. They also include the various child-directed behaviors required by our parent role. These activities, depending on the developmental stage of each child, range from primarily physical care to education and social training. The amount of energy and time we put into them is bounded only by our limitations or those we impose.

Ideally, we develop in partnership with our spouses extensive skills in guiding the development of our children and adolescents, and the relationship should produce a synergy of skills. With preschoolers and early school-age children, we learn how to encourage their caution as well as their curiosity and their attraction to people. We become adept at handling their life events: separation (being left in nursery school or kindergarten), lying and taking things that belong to others, toilet-training accidents, obedience and disobedience, and motivation and nonmotivation (laziness). When we have an intellectually gifted child, the challenges to our parenting skills increase much faster than our pride in being so fortunate. As these our children enter preadolescence and adolescence, our attention to their socialization as well as to their growth and development must *increase*, not relax. These are the years when peer groups and role models are most influential with our children. To counterbalance the influence of others, especially of unknown others, we must raise the training of our children to a yet more difficult plateau, teaching them about health and nutrition habits; the understanding of accident prevention; the understanding of alcohol, drug, and cigarette abuse; and the understanding of their sexuality.

Biologically, these preadolescent and early adolescent years are marked by the final steps in brain development which give young people cognitive potentialities not previously available to them. While they struggle with the physical changes in their bodies, with new feelings and evolving sexual tensions, and while they grapple with (even for them) unpredictable and bewildering changes in moods occurring for reasons they do not understand, these maturing children have new intellectual sensitivities and capacities to explore. Our society errs in letting them wallow their way through these extraordinary, simultaneous changes. No other society in history has been so unwise. What these young people need during their preadolescent and early adolescent years—more than at any other time in their lives—is structure and guidance.

Structure and guidance are imperative for children brought up in our society. We suffer, in the United States, from an over-abundance of material goods and of apparent choices (career opportunities, living environments, life-styles, and modes of leisure).[10] The communications media, particularly television, whip up our awareness of these choices to a high-pressured, intrusive, and sometimes almost hysterical crescendo. In such an environment, the task of defining expectations is fraught with tension, conflict, and not infrequently chronic feelings of frustration. For those of us who inhabit affluent societies, this smearing, blurring, magnification, and distortion of needs and wants by those outside the individual and family have become an albatross around our necks. Somehow, the interaction of overabundant goods and choices with the rapid social changes since World War II has produced within us strong undercurrents of existential pain. This pain is felt as isolation and loneliness by people of *all ages* and all walks of life.

Preadulthood in particular is a time of training about the media—their techniques, their content, and their motivations. These are the years when values are explored and explained. These are the years during which it is important for us parents to be criticized for being "unfair" or too strict because of the limits we set. In setting limits and in standing by them consistently, we powerfully communicate our beliefs and values. We present ourselves to our children as clearly defined individuals with a sense of ourselves, our needs, and our limitations. Growing up with such parents as reference points, being able to struggle with them over differences of opinion and desire, produces strength and health in children. They know whence they came; they know whom they love and who has loved and nurtured them. They sense how their parents cope with the many issues of life. This dual approach of setting up a family with clear boundaries yet allowing children the freedom to challenge and test those boundaries is the key to producing "alive" young adults who have a sense of things important and things of beauty and who take joy in striving (with oneself or in a system) and joy in accomplishment.

Responsible parenting, by definition, must affect our work.

The foregoing discussion only touches on some of the things that require intellectual and emotional investment on our part. Time and energy are required. Responsible parenting can no more be confined to certain hours or certain amounts than the work an executive does in meeting his or her responsibilities at work. Imagination and flexibility are absolutely necessary. The flexibility should include the willingness to take time out of work when necessary (by phone with spouse or child or in person). Here, too, limit setting is important. There are times when you cannot or do not want to allow intrusions into work, and it is important to communicate that reality to your spouse and children. Also, you should not allow this intruding into your work to become a routine, or a habit any more than you should allow work intrusions into family time to become a habit. Thus, competent parenting serves as excellent additional training in time engineering and management of personal resources in the workplace. It adds to, rather than detracts from, your executive skills. It is "transportable"!

How to Improve Your Functioning

If we want to improve our functioning we can think in terms of an ABC: This means working to refine our Attitude about parenting, our Beliefs about child rearing, and our skills in Coping. I have talked much of our attitude toward parenting in this book, about examining the personal and social importance of that role and the intellectual and even spiritual challenges it presents. Yet there exists in the upper and upper middle classes of our society a kind of fashionable cynicism about children and involvement with them. The following quote from a real mother illustrates one instance of this:

> A major problem when my baby was eight months old was that I was so bored with her. I got a stack of Piaget books to read so that at least I could find out what was going on. . . . Only that didn't work because I found Piaget even more boring than my baby.[11]

At some time each of us feels like or has fantasies of running away from parenting. Those fantasies express fatigue, stress, and the need for a break. They are OK to have. They are warning signals which should be attended to—that is, take that break. The kind of attitude expressed in the above quote by the young mother is something else again. If you truly feel that kind of negativism about parenting, your child, your family, and you are in danger. Consultation with yourself, your trusted friends, and your family physician or pediatrician is definitely warranted.

Our beliefs about child rearing are based on our knowledge and instincts about the process. The mnemonic DAFNE presented earlier recognizes some of the necessary elements. Crucial to parenting is a conviction (no matter what the child may occasionally tell you!) of the importance you have as parents. While ending a brief scolding to his ten-year-old son, a father was overheard to say, "It is our responsibility as parents to teach you these things." That father was correct. Because he knew and felt that he was right, he made several things happen by delivering that simple sentence, and those things will happen again every time that sentence is delivered. These things include the following:

1. The father was role modeling to his child, conveying to that child (and children know when you are acting and when you deeply believe what you say) the importance that he, the father, saw in his role. He was also role modeling for his son a style of being a male parent in a limit-setting situation.
2. The father was conveying values to that child.
3. The father was giving the child a sense of importance by letting him glimpse, briefly, the reality that there are reasons for authority and the exercise of power.

Coping skills for all parents, not just executive parents, are built on one's attitude and beliefs about parenting. They have as a necessary element a sense that we can attain some mystery and some control over the situations we encounter. I have already spoken of the skills of time and resource management, of listening, and of working with one's spouse. It is extremely important, too, to allow yourself to step back every now and then, to be off duty from parenting. Couples often do this by sharing in the various activities and relieving each other. Also, couples need to take time off as *couples*. (Try in-town vacations away from home as one emotionally—if you have young children—and financially less expensive form of R and R than a quick plane trip to some vacation spa.) Without individual off-duty time, without R and R taken together, the parents become so wound up by the demands of the job that they overreact as well as underreact to various situations. The joys of parenting pale, and the problems loom larger than necessary.

More subtle and just as important is the setting of limits for the *children* about your availability to them. Such limit setting teaches them to respect you as an individual person, and that respect will extend to others as well. When you're tired of a child sitting on your lap or using you as a jungle gym, put him or her gently and firmly down. Don't wait until you are so annoyed that you explode with irritability; that only serves to frighten and bewilder the child. When your son or daughter wants music lessons added to the tennis, scout, and club meetings to which you already dutifully drive them and you've had enough of such "schlepping," don't scramble around to set up another car pool. Simply say to them that they have, in your opinion, quite enough activities and that more driving would leave you too little time for your own needs and activities. There are several messages delivered simultaneously in such a stand, and not one of them is a nonloving, noncaring message. It is not only OK for parents to say no, it is often necessary.

Learning how to spend leisure time (yours and theirs) can be a hurdle for many parents. Avoid at all costs those forced "Daddy is available Sunday, let's go somewhere" family excursions. Both for parents and children, they never quite "taste" right in retrospect, even with a retrospect of years. Everyone gets into a mind set about being dutiful and responsible to everyone else (being a good child, a caring parent, etc.). Where there is such engineered togetherness, spontaneity and joyfulness go by the boards. If your work makes you regularly available only on Sundays when others in the family are available too, simply make it known. Everyone should be frank about what they need to do. If it is something to be done together, make the choice together. As often as not, some of the greatest pleasures may be experienced in simply being around one another without pressures or plans or expectations.

Being of the executive class confers certain economic privileges, not the least of which is the opportunity to employ baby-sitters, housekeepers, and other outside assistance. This assistance can be used to buffer us somewhat from the extra pressures that we impose on ourselves. (Though let's not kid ourselves, these pressures and stresses are in no way comparable to those felt by the unskilled or low-skilled father or mother who is working two jobs just to keep the family economically viable.) Appropriate, reasonably free use of outside helpers not only contributes to employment, it can also be cost-effective for the parents. Isn't it better to pay a housekeeper than to pay a psychotherapist or marriage therapist because you were too busy to relax, change pace, and talk with your spouse?

Another major coping skill which all of us can improve on is humor. By definition, when there is humor we are able to step back from ourselves and from the intensity of our involvements. It is a good thing to teach our children, for it adds to human tensile strength. Teaching humor occurs only through experiencing it. Fortunately, there is much humor about both work and parenting in our culture. We need only relax to see the funny side of things. As my secretary said to me not long ago: "We're having growing pains in our family. My son is growing and I'm having the pain!"

Interactions within the family give us messages all the time about how well we are coping. But an important coping skill includes not limiting ourselves to the family. Parenting is something of our culture and communities, too. Go beyond yourself and spouse. Grandparents are resources; friends are resources. Sometimes even casually encountered strangers when kept at an appropriate distance can be helpful: One recent study revealed that 14 percent of mothers who went to a pediatrician about a behavioral problem with their child found that they received useful help from someone other than the pediatrician.[12] Perhaps it was the parent sitting next to them in the waiting room!

MANAGEMENT OF YOUR LIFE SYSTEM

Five questions were posed at the beginning of this book:

- How much time should be spent with work and work-related activities?

- How much time should be spent with the family?
- How does one relate family to work?
- How much time can one afford for exercise, for leisure, and for community activities?
- Is it all right, given all these demands, to have a nonstructured leisure, occasionally—to just loaf or wander or sit?

Since posing these questions, I have talked about input overload, limit setting, honoring the family as a refuge, stress, guilt, divorce, separation, and many other topics. Suggestions about how to approach certain situations and selected strategies for coping with them have been presented. Where does this take you, "the executive–the parent"?

Let me quote from Bruno Bettelheim's book *The Uses of Enchantment*: "A unified personality able to meet successfully, with inner security, the difficulties of living. Inner integration . . . is a task that confronts us all our lives."[13] That's correct: The task confronts us all our lives. We are ever changing as are those around us. This changing creates part of the excitement in the challenges of life! My specific answer and your specific answer to those five original questions should change from moment to moment in our lives.

Wait! I am not "copping out." For you, for me, and for others, a general answer can be given to each question. Those answers should be useful reference points.

- Spending time with work does not present a problem for executives. Rather, the decision involves the setting of limits and leaving enough time for community. ("A community is a group of people with ties to each other, ties of kinship and friendship, ties of shared work and shared responsibility and shared pleasure. The nucleus of any community is people who know and value each other"[14] [Margaret Mead].) Time with work must be traded against the time one is really spending with family and children. If time with them becomes a very limited or even an occasional thing, you have gone overboard in what you are devoting to work. Remember to use, as one friend so wisely advised me a long time ago when I was struggling with input overload, the "twenty-year test"; that is, reflect on the meaning and importance of the work you are doing now as you might judge it twenty years hence, and you will discover that probably 90 percent of what you are doing has little meaning and no importance in that perspective.

- Family is where we begin. If we are fortunate, it is where we will end. Without it we are indeed limited creatures. Time and significant amounts of it should always exist for family.
- Family and work—work and family—should be related to each other. Because they simply no longer have the same intimate relationship that existed in the nineteenth century does not mean that they should be alienated from one another. It does mean that extra efforts are needed to keep the two mutually supportive of each other and to keep us from being divided.
- Those incapable of self-care are less capable of caring for others. Self-care is not synonymous with self-indulgence. Time for exercise and leisure benefits the executive–the parent and the system for which he or she has responsibility.
- "Doing nothing" means allowing time for being, for noticing and enjoying. Time for doing nothing must be made. Without it we lose our capacity for wonder, human sharing, and growth of spirit.

THE FUTURE SIGNIFICANCE
OF YOUR BEHAVIORS

If you paid no attention to this before joining me in this book, you certainly are now aware that throughout our society families exist that could be described as "households full of strangers." The parents within them eventually separate or divorce, bitter about their mistake in marrying or about their failure in marriage. Not infrequently, at least one of their children is doing poorly in school; has run away; or is involved in vandalism, sexual acting out, or drug or alcohol abuse. One wonders at such households, particularly if they are headed by the highly educated and privileged. Consider such a household whose head is an executive. How could the described dysfunctions have developed? Isn't the well-functioning executive "confident, competent, open-minded"?[15] Trained and/or selected for ability to focus attention, relate to people, control their own impulses, and identify problems early and approach them from a problem-oriented perspective, executives have tremendous potential as family leaders. It is necessary to mobilize and use these potentials in our private lives.

Until recently it could reasonably be said that issues of the family were considered by organizations to have little to no relevance to the functioning of these organizations. "Management seems unable to envisage any other approach to organization-family interactions than the usual one of ignoring one system, usually the family system. Only when the stresses become unbearable are the interactions recognized."[16]

Over the past couple of years, the importance of family to work and of work to family—their being part of a system in terms of their effects on one another—has been recognized both by the public and private sectors. Just a few specific examples include the following:

- The establishment of the Family Liaison Office by a major department in the executive branch of the federal government. This office, established by Secretary of State Cyrus Vance in 1977, resides at the level of the assistant secretary of state for management. Vance's enthusiastic sponsorship and that of his wife have continued. The office itself thrives in its work as an advocate and helper for Foreign Service officers' families and senior-level Department of State employees.
- The creation of a community mental health center—the Social Development Center—in Teheran, Iran, as an experiment on behalf of American families. The center concentrated its activities on family problems. A number of multinational corporations contributed to the center's support.
- The Aspen Institute for Humanistic Studies, famous for its Executive Seminar Program, began to hold meetings entitled "The Corporation and the Family." The discussions at these meetings included: "The place of the family in society (and) ways in which corporations affect the family."[17]

The above examples show recognition of the need to change the way we think about families.

Executives are among those with special status in the American community. That status means that the greater community attributes to executives degrees of influence, authority, and even power that are not attributed to many others. This, in turn, means that executives, through the values they express by their life-styles, can influence the values and life-styles of others. Sociologists call this the "principle of stratified diffusion;" and they explain it in the following fashion: "Many social changes start at the top and work downwards. The people in the van of the column . . . foreshadow what those at the rear will be doing tomorrow, just as those at the rear represent the past of those ahead of them."[18] As you see, we are not dealing with elitism. Rather, the process of role modeling of groups is quite real and quite demonstrable in most societies throughout history.

Families are as key to the continuity of our social system as is parenting to the continuity of our species. Today, maintaining a family and performing with confidence and pleasure in the parent role represent a considerable challenge. That challenge can be met, however. Your enthusiastic and thoughtful involvement as parents within families, when combined with the successful pursuit of your executive careers, will have a powerful, enriching effect on more than your own lives. It will have a stabilizing effect on our society as a whole.

APPENDIX A

Resources in Print

The books in this brief annotated bibliography are listed by subject area. I present them as selected works which may be of help and interest to you.

GENERAL HEALTH CARE OF CHILDREN

The following book should not intimidate you by being called an "Encyclopaedia"—it is only one volume. Written by health professionals, this volume is the most thorough, caring book I know of written expressly for parents. The information contained is of the highest quality on all aspects of health and ill health, including accidents in children. The language used is straightforward and easy to follow.

The Boston Children's Medical Center and Richard I. Feinbloom, M.D. *Child Health Encyclopaedia: The Complete Guide for Parents.* New York: Delacorte Press, Seymour Lawrence, 1975.

149

CHILD DEVELOPMENT AND PARENTING

The first of the books recommended here was written by the same group that produced the *Child Health Encyclopaedia*. It is a comprehensive, clearly written book covering the prenatal, birth, and just postbirth periods. I suggest looking for its most recent edition, since attitudes on the part of the medical profession have changed somewhat in recent years.

The next two books are written by one of the country's most gifted practicing pediatricians, who also engages in high-quality, innovative research and public education. These books are of special importance as in-depth illustrations of the temperamental differences of children and parents; Dr. Brazelton fills both volumes with wise advice and guidance.

It is most difficult to find general books on parenting that are high-spirited, wise, and easy to read. It is almost incredible to think that a committee could write such a book, but that is indeed what one has in the slim volume entitled *The Joys and Sorrows of Parenthood.*

Other than lecturing our children or spanking them, how does one deal with lying, teasing, or other such problems during the school years? I have had such questions as a parent, as I am sure you have had. Dr. Gardner's small volume answers such questions by taking you by the hand and actually showing you how to handle such situations through the recounting of stories to your children. I highly recommend it.

Finally, you may wonder about a book on adolescence. Obviously, many have been written over the years. Some of the best popular presentations (for their insight and wisdom) were delivered by Dr. Fritz Redl from the late 1930s through the 1960s. I cannot, however, recommend any one book to you.

The Boston Children's Medical Center. *Pregnancy, Birth, and the Newborn Baby.* New York: Delacorte Press, Seymour Lawrence, 1972.

T. Berry Brazelton. *Infants and Mothers: Differences in Development.* New York: Delacorte Press, 1969.

T. Berry Brazelton. *Toddlers and Parents: A Declaration of Independence.* New York: Delacorte Press, 1975.

Group for the Advancement of Psychiatry. *The Joys and Sorrows of Parenthood.* Vol. 3, report no. 80. New York: 1973.

Richard A. Gardner, M. D. *Dr. Gardner's Stories about the Real World.* Englewood Cliffs, N.J.: Prentice-Hall, 1972.

SOME SPECIAL SITUATIONS

Adoption

The following book, based on a research study, deals with the primary issue before all adoptive parents today. This issue is that of reunion—the legal, social, and personal questions concerning adopted children seeking their biologic parents and biologic parents seeking their adopted children.

Arthur D. Sorosky, Annette Baran, and Reuben Pannor. *The Adoption Triangle.* Garden City, N.Y.: Anchor Press, 1978.

Death

As mentioned in my discussion on death and loss, both subjects often relate to each other from the psychological and social points of view. The following books deal only with the issue of death. Most popular of them is Elisabeth Kübler-Ross's book, which has become a classic. I would warn you about taking too literally her presentation of the stages of dying. These are reasonable generalizations, but we are very complicated creatures and do not do things in sequence; that is not our psychosocial makeup. I warn you on this subject because I have experienced as a clinician families and individuals who have taken her book too literally, almost as a "cookbook," and have suffered confusion and distress as a result. I am quite sure that Dr. Kübler-Ross never meant her book to be taken in that fashion.

The Eda LeShan book is for children who have lost a parent. Reviewers find it to be also useful for any adult, parent, or teacher, as well as for children, who are simply interested in the subject of death. The William Easson book is of general interest. It provides a reasonable and readable summary of issues when a child or adolescent is him- or herself faced with death. Finally, Dr. Shneidman's book is one of the most sensitive and reasonable as well as most well-written tomes on the entire subject of death and loss in our society.

Elisabeth Kübler-Ross. *On Death And Dying.* New York: Macmillan Company, 1969.

Eda LeShan. *Learning to Say Goodbye.* New York: Macmillan Company, 1976.

William M. Easson. *The Dying Child.* Springfield, Ill.: Charles C. Thomas, 1970.

Edwin S. Shneidman. *Deaths of Man.* New York: Quadrangle Books, 1973.

Divorce and Separation

The following two books are practical, thorough, and without jargon. The first book is written for school-age children and young adolescents; it should simultaneously be read by their parents.

Richard A. Gardner, M.D. *The Boys and Girls Book About Divorce.* New York: Jason Aronson, 1970.

Richard A. Gardner, M.D. *The Parents Book About Divorce.* Garden City, N.Y.: Doubleday and Company, 1977.

Mental Retardation

There are many books on the subject of mental retardation. The following one was not written for the layperson. However, I am so impressed with the information contained and the issues raised that I believe it is worth the attention of any parent particularly interested in the subject, no matter what reason he or she may have.

Michael J. Begab and Stephen A. Richardson, eds. *The Mentally Retarded and Society: A Social Science Perspective.* Baltimore: University Park Press, 1975.

Other Handicapping Conditions

The following book is an example of the kind of written material we need more of. It is written both for the exceptional child and for his or her parents. Indeed, half of the book is written for the child and the other half is written for the parent. Real-life situations are presented with suggested ways for dealing with them.

Richard A. Gardner, M.D. *The Family Book About Minimal Brain Dysfunction.* New York: Jason Aronson, 1973.

Moving to Other Countries

The author of the following book has had extensive experience in working with government and private-sector families who for reasons of work must leave the United States and settle in other places. Even when these other places are Paris, Rome, and London, the process is more challenging than the uninitiated might think. Especially when your work assignment takes you to Kabul or the Central African Republic, you would be wise to educate yourselves and do as much planning in advance as possible. I suggest reading Dr. Werkman's book as simply the first general step. He is down-to-earth, raising major issues for your consideration and presenting specific advice.

Sidney Werkman, M.D. *Bring Up Children Overseas: A Guide for Families.* New York: Basic Books, 1977.

BOOKS OF GENERAL INTEREST

For the executive parent of the early 1980s, I strongly suggest sharing in the observations and perspectives presented by the following two books. The first, written by Kenneth Keniston and the Carnegie Council on Children, pulls together information and insights based on an intense study of children and families in the United States. Neither lengthy nor ponderous, the book presents issues worthy of all our attention. The second book, by the well-known child psychiatrist Dr. Robert Coles, provides insights into a select number of children of the privileged class in different parts of the country. Dr. Coles's studies are done not in libraries but by spending hours with the children and their families. Because of his method, his perspectives provide a special resource for all of us.

Kenneth Keniston and the Carnegie Council on Children. *All Our Children: The American Family Under Pressure.* New York: Harcourt Brace Jovanovich, 1977.

Robert Coles. *Privileged Ones.* Vol. 5 of *Children of Crisis.* Boston: Little, Brown and Company, 1977.

APPENDIX B

Resources for Special Situations

SEEKING PROFESSIONAL HELP

Even professionals find it a challenge to select for themselves or their families individuals who will provide care of high quality with high integrity. This does not mean that many superb professionals of all the disciplines do not exist throughout the country. They do—whether your needs are simply for a routine physical examination or for psychotherapy. The problem is how to locate them. Most professionals of all disciplines are clustered in cities or in urban areas; the more rural the area, the fewer choices and disciplines you have available to you.

Individuals who deliver health care, mental health care, and even family and marital counseling need to be licensed in almost all jurisdictions of this country. Such licensing provides the consumer with a baseline, but only a baseline, assurance of quality. Recommendations from respected friends, relatives, or

155

colleagues who have had direct experience with the individual they are recommending provide further initial screening. In all communities, the local medical societies maintain lists of members according to their areas of specialization and special interests. Names are available to the public on request. Some medical societies list individuals according to location within the community, whether or not they accept various kinds of third-party insurance, and their abilities in different languages. By using the phone book, you can check to see if there is a branch of the medical society, the American Academy of Pediatrics, the American Academy of Child Psychiatry, the American Psychiatric Association, and the American Psychological Association in your area. All of them can give you some help by at least providing the names of individuals. For mental health problems, the local branches of the Mental Health Association throughout the country can often prove helpful, providing information on local resources—be they clinics or private practitioners.

Again, realize that seeking appropriate professional help is a process that does take time, effort, and the exercise of *your judgment* and *common sense.* Even if you are a member of a group health association that provides counseling as well as health care, you should always be most frank in your questions and questioning. If you have trouble communicating with the health professional or counselor, it may not be *your* problem. You have a right and indeed the responsibility to yourself and your family to have all things explained to you *in language that you can understand.* Don't worry about whether you are taking too much of the helping professional's time. You're seeing them to have *your* needs met. If there is a dispute about your taking too much time or being inappropriate, that is for you and the health professional to work out together. The best trained of health professionals are sensitive to these dimensions of patient-doctor and client–health worker interactions and are trained to deal with them appropriately (that is, helpfully).

VOLUNTARY ORGANIZATIONS ASSOCIATED WITH SPECIAL CAUSES OR CONDITIONS

Below are listed some of the voluntary organizations which can provide significant assistance to parents and families who are beset by certain problems. Besides being involved in community and political action, these organizations have gone extensively into promoting high-quality information about the conditions in question and resources for dealing with them. All the associations listed are well established. Executive directors and addresses do change, but the following list of addresses is current as of January 1979. The organizations are listed under the general description of the conditions they serve.

Autism

National Society for Autistic Children
1234 Massachusetts Avenue, N.W. Suite 1017
Washington, DC 20005
(202) 783-1025

Cancer

The Candlelighters
123 C Street, S.E.
Washington, DC 20003
(202) 483-9100 or 544-1696

Cerebral Palsy

United Cerebral Palsy Associations, Inc.
66 E. 34th Street
New York, NY 10036
(212) 481-6300

Congenital Heart Disease

American Heart Association
2233 Wisconsin Avenue, N.W.
Washington, DC 20007
(212) 337-6400

Dysautonomia

Dysautonomia Foundation, Inc.
370 Lexington Avenue, Room 1508
New York, NY 10016
(212) 889-0300

Hearing Impaired

American Speech, Language and Hearing Association
10801 Rockville Pike
Rockville, MD 20856
(301) 897-5700

Genetic Diseases

The National Genetics Foundation, Inc.
9 West 57th Street
New York, NY 10019
(212) 759-4432

Learning Disabilities

American Association for Children With Learning Disabilities
4156 Library Road
Pittsburgh, PA 15234
(412) 341-1515

Mental Health Problems

Mental Health Association
1800 North Kent Street
Arlington, VA 22209
(703) 528-6405

Mental Retardation

National Association for Retarded Citizens
2709 Avenue "E"
East Arlington, TX 76011
(817) 261-4961

Seizure Disorders

Epilepsy Foundation of America
1828 L Street, N.W. Suite 406
Washington, DC 20036
(202) 293-2930

Sudden Infant Death Syndrome (Crib Death)

National Foundation for Sudden Infant Death
310 S. Michigan Avenue
Chicago, IL 60604
(312) 663-0659

Visually Impaired

American Foundation for the Blind
15 West 16th Street
New York, NY 10011
(212) 620-2000

SELF-HELP GROUPS

Literally hundreds of self-help groups exist throughout the country at this time. Many of them have developed out of existing voluntary organizations. Examples include the self-help groups found associated with the National Hemophilia Foundation, the National Society for Autistic Children, the Candlelighters, and the National Multiple Sclerosis Foundation. A large number of such organizations are organized around problems. Sometimes they are organized around challenges to coping, such as the National Organization of Mothers of Twins Clubs, or around issues of life-style, such as the National Organization for Non-Parents. In other cases they are a combination of advocacy, community, and political action organizations. The best example in terms of its level of activity and success is Ms. Peggy Charren's Action for Children's Television. Some would not see such a group as involving self-help. This does raise the issue of where self-help ends and community action begins. When one looks at the history of these organizations, such borders are frequently crossed many times.

One source of information on the self-help groups in the United States is National Self-Help Clearinghouse, Graduate School and University Center, City University of New York, 33 W. 42nd Street, Room 1227, New York, NY 10036.

Self-help groups are not fixed entities. They are something

created by people for themselves and their families in times of need. When they promote the integrity and autonomy of individual families and people and when they simultaneously seek the best information available on the issue of concern, they are important additions to our community. They should serve as community workshops that promote coping and tolerance; they should work toward the reduction of stigma. If you become involved in one and it *does not have* these characteristics as primary elements, I strongly recommend that you reconsider your continued participation in the group.

Notes

PREFACE

1. *Characteristics of American Children and Youth: 1976.* Current Population Reports, Special Studies Series P-23, no. 66, U.S. Department of Commerce, Bureau of the Census, 1978, p. 40.
2. Margaret Mead. *Redbook*, February 1977, p. 161.

CHAPTER 1

1. Edith H. Grotberg, ed. *Two Hundred Years of Children.* U.S. Department of Health, Education and Welfare (GPO Stock Number 017-090-0029-1), 1977.
2. Mary Cabel. *The Little Darlings: A History of Childrearing in America.* New York: Charles Scribner's Sons, 1975, p. 192.
3. Michael Maccoby. *The Gamesman.* New York: Simon & Schuster, 1976.
4. Christy Brown. *The Story of Christy Brown* (original title, *My Left Foot*). New York: Simon & Schuster, 1971, pp. 12–13.
5. Kenneth Keniston and the Carnegie Council on Children. *All Our*

Children: The American Family Under Pressure. New York: Harcourt Brace Jovanovich, 1977, pp. 12 and 17.

CHAPTER 2

1. These time and work data were obtained from the U.S. Department of Commerce.
2. This material is adapted from my own clinical work and from the article: Barrie S. Greiff, M.D. "The Executive Family Seminar: A Course for Graduate Married Business Students." *Journal of the American College Health Association* 24 (1976): 227–231.
3. Chester R. Barnard. *The Functions of the Executive.* Cambridge: Harvard University Press, 1942, pp. 215–216.
4. The phrases "sustaining environment" and "nurturing environment" originally came from Dr. Leon Chestang, professor of sociology at the University of Chicago. Further insights for commentary on minority executives came from the book: James P. Comer, M.D. *Beyond Black and White.* New York: Quadrangle Books, 1972.
5. Clifton Bryant, ed. *The Social Dimensions of Work.* Englewood Cliffs, N.J.: Prentice-Hall, 1972.
6. According to the National Institute of Alcohol Abuse and Alcoholism, over 200,000 executives currently engage in irresponsible use of alcohol.
7. This passage refers to physical abuse, or the "battered wives" syndrome. Although one can see a similar phenomenon involving women battering men, in our culture the most common occurrences by far involve men physically abusing women. Refuges have now been established in various communities for women fleeing their husbands. An example is the House of Ruth in Washington, D.C. This phenomenon is by no means found only in the lower socioeconomic classes.
8. Those in the executive class find themselves in the top 5 to 10 percent of incomes, commanding with others in that bracket at least half the resources of our society.
9. Percy E. Davidson and H. Dewey Anderson. *Occupational Trends.* Stanford: Stanford University Press, 1940, p. 1. The commentary on stress and coping is based on my clinical and teaching experience as well as: G. V. Coelho, D. A. Hamburg, and John E. Adams, eds., *Coping and Adaptation.* New York: Basic Books, 1974.

CHAPTER 3

1. *The American Heritage Dictionary of the English Language: New College Edition.* Boston: Houghton Mifflin Co., 1976.
2. François Mauriac. *The Knot of Vipers.* Translated by Gerard Hopkins. London: Eyre and Spottiswood, 1956.
3. M. Harvey Brenner. *Mental Illness and the Economy.* Cambridge: Harvard University Press, 1973. Cited in the *Congressional Record* S. 78, January 1976
4. Stephen P. Hersh and Karen Levin. "How Love Begins Between Parent and Child." *Children Today,* Vol. 7, no. 2 (1978).
5. Alexander Thomas, Stella Chess and Herbert G. Birch. *Temperament and Behavior Disorders in Children.* New York: New York University Press, 1968.
6. Nancy Aidei and Theodora Ooms. "Toward an Inventory of Federal Programs Which Have Impacts on Families: Background Notes for the Family Impact Seminar." Unpublished report, George Washington University, Washington, D.C. November 16–17, 1976.
7. *The American Heritage Dictionary of the English Language.*
8. Theodore Lidz. *The Person.* New York: Basic Books, 1968, pp. 45–46.
9. Theodore Lidz. *The Family and Human Adaptation.* New York: International Universities Press, 1963, p. 47.
10. The data in this section come from: *Current Population Reports: Population Characteristics,* Series P-20, nos. 311 and 313 (1977) and no. 323 (1978), Bureau of the Census. And *Characteristics of American Children and Youth: 1976,* Special Studies Series P-23, no. 66 (1978), U.S. Department of Commerce, Bureau of the Census.
11. Parts of this section are adapted from: S. P. Hersh and Ira S. Lourie. "Youth, Behavior, and Social Change." In *Basic Handbook of Child Psychiatry,* edited by J. Noshpitz. New York: Basic Books, (forthcoming).
12. R. Buckminster Fuller. "Cutting the Metabilical Chord." *Saturday Review,* 21 October 1974.
13. Richard I. Feinbloom. "T.V. Update." *Pediatrics* 62, no. 3 (1978): 428–431.
14. Ibid., 430.
15. I am indebted to Leslie Scallet, J.D., for summary materials on children's rights issues used by me in preparing this section.
16. Paul L. Adams. "The Legacy of Child-Murder." Unpublished pa-

per, 1977. (Professor and Vice-Chairperson, Department of Psychiatry and Behavioral Sciences, University of Louisville School of Medicine, Louisville, Kentucky). Quoted with permission.

CHAPTER 4

1. Antoine de Sainte-Exupery. *The Little Prince.* New York: Harcourt, Brace and World, 1973, dedication page.
2. Elizabeth M. R. Lomax in collaboration with Jerome Kagen and Barbara G. Rosenkrantz. "Science and the Myths of Child Rearing." Unpublished study, Washington, D.C., Assembly of Life Sciences, National Research Council, National Academy of Sciences, 1977, p. 167.
3. Stephen P. Hersh and Karen Levin. "How Love Begins Between Parent and Child." *Children Today,* Vol. 7, no. 2, (1978).
4. Herbert Yahraes. "Parents as Leaders: The Role of Controlling Discipline." A chapter based on the work of Diana Baumrind and colleagues, University of California at Berkeley, in a volume on the family, in preparation 1977-78 by the Mental Health Science Reports Branch, Division of Scientific and Public Information, National Institute of Mental Health, U.S. Public Health Service, 1978.
5. George F. Will. "Loco Parentis." *Washington Post,* 13 February 1977.
6. Leo Kanner. *Child Psychiatry.* 3rd ed. Springfield, Ill.: Charles C. Thomas, 1962, p. 170.
7. Paul Chodoff, M.D. Personal communication, 1977.
8. *The Joys and Sorrows of Parenthood,* Vol. 3, report no. 80. Committee on Public Education, Group for the Advancement of Psychiatry. New York, 1973, p. 261.
9. Diana Baumrind, Ph.D. Quoted in: Herbert Yahraes. "Parents as Leaders." Unpublished study, division of Scientific and Public Information, National Institute of Mental Health, U.S. Public Health Service, 1978.

CHAPTER 5

1. "The Changing Family." *Wilson Quarterly* 1, no. 1 (1977), 79.
2. *Marital Status and Living Arrangements: March 1977.* Current Population Reports: Population Characteristics, Series P-20, no. 323, (April 1978). U.S. Department of Commerce, Bureau of the Census.
3. *Marriage and Divorce Today.* New York: Atcom.

4. Report on studies of Dr. Robert Michael, Department of Economics, Stanford University, in the *National Bureau of Economic Research Reporter*, December 1977.
5. *Marital Status and Living Arrangements: March 1977.*
6. Roberta Kingston. Program prospectus of the Rubicon Women's Project, Services for Battered Women, 1978.
7. Rabbi Eårl A. Grollman and Marjorie L. Sams. *Living Through Your Divorce.* Boston: Beacon Press, 1977.
8. David R. Offord, Nancy Allen, and Nola Abrams. "Parental Psychiatric Illness, Broken Homes, and Delinquency." *Journal of Child Psychiatry* 17 (1978): 224–238.
9. J. S. Wallerstein and J. B. Kelly. "The Effects of Parental Divorce: The Adolescent Experience." In *The Child in His Family: Children at Psychiatric Risk*, edited by J. Anthony and C. Koupernik. New York: John Wiley and Sons, 1974. Also in J. S. Wallerstein and J. B. Kelly, "The Effects of Parental Divorce: Experiences of the Preschool Child." *Journal of Child Psychiatry* 14 (1975): 660–616.
10. Jeanne Spurlock and Karen Rembold. "Women at Fault: Societal Stereotypes and Clinical Conclusions." *Journal of Child Psychiatry* 17 (1978): 387–388.
11. Richard S. Benedek and Elissa P. Benedek. "Post Divorce Visitation." *Journal of Child Psychiatry* 16 (1977): 256–271.
12. John F. McDermott. "Parental Divorce and Early Childhood." *American Journal of Psychiatry* 124 (1968): 1424–1432.
13. Richard A. Gardner, M.D. *The Boys and Girls Book About Divorce.* New York: Jason Aronson, 1970, p. 55.
14. *Federal Research Activity in Mental Retardation.* Report of the Ad Hoc Consultants on Mental Retardation. U.S. Public Health Service, National Institute of Mental Health and Human Development, Department of Health, Education and Welfare. February 1977, p. 1.
15. Task Panel Reports Submitted to the President's Commission on Mental Health. In *Mental Health in American Families*, Vol. 3 (Appendix). Washington, D.C.: Government Printing Office, 1978, p. 595.
16. Third Special Report to the U.S. Congress on *Alcohol and Health*, from the secretary of the Department of Health, Education, and Welfare. Edited by Ernest P. Noble, Ph.D., M.D. National Institute on Alcohol Abuse and Alcoholism, June 1978. Other factual materials in this section are derived from this report.
17. Ibid.
18. Edith H. Grotberg, ed. *Two Hundred Years of Children.* U.S. De-

partment of Health, Education and Welfare Publication, no. (OHD) 77-30103, 1977.
19. Sidney Werkman, M.D. *Bringing Up Children Overseas.* New York: Basic Books, 1977.
20. Robert Coles. *Privileged Ones.* Vol. 5 of *Children of Crisis.* Boston: Little, Brown and Company, 1977, p. 550.
21. Ibid., p. 553.
22. Sylvia Anthony. "The Child's Idea of Death." In *The World of the Child*, edited by Toby Talbot. New York: Jason Aronson, 1974, pp. 315–328.
23. George W. Brown. "Depression and Loss." *British Journal of Psychiatry* 130 (1977): 1–18.
24. Mark Twain. Quoted in: Edwin S. Shneidman. *Deaths of Man.* New York: Quadrangle, 1973, p. 218.
25. Ibid., p. 219.
26. Richard E. Sorenson. *The Edge of the Forest: Land, Childhood, and Change in a New Guinea Protoagricultural Society.* Washington, D.C.: Smithsonian Institution Press, 1976.
27. George V. Coelho and Jane J. Stein. "Coping With Stresses of an Urban Planet." U.S. Department of Health, Education and Welfare Publication, no. (ADM) 78-609, 1978. Originally printed in *Habitat: An International Journal*, Vol. 2, no. 1, London: Pergamon Press, 1977.
28. Sidney Werkman, M.D. *Bringing Up Children Overseas: A Guide for Families.* New York: Basic Books, 1977.
29. Gerald Caplan and Marie Killilea, eds. *Support Systems and Mutual Help: Multidisciplinary Exploration.* New York: Grune and Stratton, 1976.
30. Ibid.
31. Ibid.
32. Divorced Kids is a self-help group that was established in Lexington, Massachusetts. It is under the general supervision of Mr. Howard Schoenfield of the Guidance Department of Lexington High School.

CHAPTER 6

1. Michael Maccoby, *The Gamesman*, New York: Simon & Schuster, 1976, p. 196.
2. Ibid., p. 193.
3. Walter S. Neff. "Work and Human History." In *The Social Di-*

mensions of Work, edited by Clifton D. Bryant. Englewood Cliffs, N.J.: Prentice-Hall, 1972, p. 51.

4. Coalition for Optional Parenting, 2233 Wisconsin Avenue, NW, Suite 322, Washington, DC 20007.
5. Michael Maccoby. *The Gamesman*, p. 197.
6. Michael Radetsky. "Recapturing the Spirit of Medicine." *New England Journal of Medicine* 298 (1978): 1142.
7. This statement is derived from a review of the literature by Henry Biller: "Father-Child Relationship: Some Crucial Issues." In *The Family—Can it Be Saved?*, edited by Victor C. Vaughan, III, and T. Berry Brazelton. Chicago: Year Book Medical Publishers, 1976. The information is also derived from various pilot studies of the mental health problems found in pediatricians' practices.
8. Jeanne R. Renshaw. "An Exploration of the Dynamics of the Overlapping Worlds of Work and Family." *Family Process* 15 (1976): 147.
9. Theodore Lidz. *The Person.* New York: Basic Books, 1968, p. 454.
10. Z. J. Lipowski. "The Conflict of Buriden's Ass, or Some Dilemmas of Affluence: The Theory of Attractive Stimulus Overload." *American Journal of Psychiatry* 127 (1970): 273–279.
11. Virginia Barber and Merrill Maguire Skaggs. *The Mother Person.* New York: Bobbs-Merrill, 1975, p. 133.
12. "The Future of Pediatric Education." A Report by the Task Force on Pediatric Education, American Academy of Pediatrics, 1978, p. 102.
13. Bruno Bettelheim, *The Uses of Enchantment.* New York: Alfred A. Knopf, 1976, p. 90.
14. Margaret Mead. "New Towns to Set New Life-Styles." In *New Towns: Why and for Whom?*, edited by Harvey S. Perloff and Neil C. Sandberg. New York: Praeger, 1973, p. 120.
15. Michael Maccoby. *The Gamesman*, p. 193.
16. Jeanne R. Renshaw. "An Exploration of the Dynamics of the Overlapping Worlds of Work and Family," p. 154.
17. Aspen Institute of Humanistic Studies, calendar no. 12, 1978.
18. Michael Young and Peter Willmott. *The Symmetrical Family.* New York: Pantheon Books, 1973, p. 33.

Index